HOW NOT TO BE A STUPID MANAGER

By

THOM K. COPE, J.D.

This edition is dedicated to my wife Melba, an inspirational, tireless advocate against discrimination. It is also dedicated to the victims of discrimination with the hope that the use of this book will help eliminate inequality in the workplace. And finally I dedicate this to all current and aspiring leaders in business: may you always do the right thing as you lead your employees.

CONTENTS

PART ONE: DOING IT RIGHT

PART TWO: EVALUATING WHAT IS AT STAKE

PREFACE

This book was originally entitled, "The Executive Guide to Employment Practices" 3rd edition. However, I have re-titled it, because in my 40 years practicing employment law, I have found that managers do stupid things leading to legal liability. I hope this book will keep you from doing stupid things, because here you will find the knowledge to avoid doing those things.

Many books have been written about Equal Employment Opportunity law, discrimination cases, and management techniques in general. Many managers have read about the law and the process of preventing discrimination charges. However, in the hundreds of management seminars that I've given around the country, these same corporate executives, human resource professionals, managers and supervisors have complained that the books they read were too technical and did not give practical "how to" advice. Also, many books didn't give enough legal explanation for managers to understand why they needed to act in a certain way. Therefore, this book is written in everyday language that explains the legal basis of conduct, which will, in many instances, prevent problems from arising.

This book is for guidance and reference purposes only. Because the book is for leaders and not lawyers, I have not included a table of cases. It is of a general informational and educational nature, and warranties of merchantability or fitness for a particular purpose are specifically excluded. This book is sold with the understanding that neither the author nor the publisher is engaged in rendering legal advice with this book. State laws vary so it is important that you contact an attorney for state specific advice. Employers facing significant decisions about legal issues and questions concerning employment or labor law should consult an attorney well versed in that jurisdiction's legal precedent.

ACKNOWLEDGMENTS

It is always appropriate to acknowledge those who have helped one to achieve a certain goal. Many people helped this edition to come to life. I would like particularly like to thank Susan Mizner who was instrumental in formatting the manuscript so I could edit it for this edition, as well as my secretary, Laura, and paralegal Becky Hunsaker at the Mesch, Clark & Rothschild law firm who proofread the final manuscript. Their suggestions were invaluable. I am also grateful to the many judges, employers, clients and colleagues from whom I gained the knowledge and insights revealed herein. Finally, I would be remiss if I didn't thank countless friends and colleagues who reviewed various parts of the book and gave me valuable assistance.

INTRODUCTION

"Nobody gets up by putting other people down!"

You may wonder why I would change the title of this book for the fourth edition. The reason is simple: managers do stupid things and cost their employers hundreds of thousands of dollars a year as a result. As examples, let me share with you just three cases I recently handled that illustrate this point.

A Hispanic construction worker went into the shop/office, went into the bathroom, locked the door to the stall and proceeded. His supervisor followed him in, stood on the toilet in the next stall and using his cell phone, took a picture of his employee sitting there. He then showed the picture of the employee on the toilet to other employees, who all got a big chuckle out of it. The affected worker found out and was not amused. He went to HR, and was told this wasn't National Origin discrimination, nor was this sex harassment and they couldn't help him. He just needed to "get over it." So he filed a discrimination charge with the state EEO agency. In defending the case, I found that the supervisor denied the event, even though over 10 people saw the picture. He was fired for lying. The case was dismissed, but not before the company spent over $3000 in defense costs. Eventually, they did what they should have done, and issued the employee an apology. Stupid manager, right?

A female employee dropped some paper on the floor. As she bent over to pick it up, her supervisor took a picture of her backside with his cell phone, downloaded it to his computer, printed it and posted it on the bulletin board. The employee was very offended and complained to the HR manager, who called me. We dealt with the situation, apologized to the employee, and then had to craft a cell phone use policy prohibiting this use. Stupid manager, right?

I represented a medical provider who fired two employees for "stealing." They were both exempt employees, but had called the payroll provider and told them they were now non-exempt and eligible for overtime. After about $25,000 of unauthorized overtime was paid, the owner figured it out. He fired the two, but then both he and his wife told everyone who would listen that the fired employees were "thieves and embezzlers." Perhaps this was true, but they were sued for defamation by these employees. Even though they could show no damage to their reputation, they demanded over $300,000 each to settle the case. The owners refused to settle and the case went to trial. The jury gave each ex-employee $1000 as "nominal damages." However defense costs were close to $50,000. What was a simple termination, turned into a two-year court battle, which could have been avoided by making no comment about the terminated employees to anyone. I recommend that approach.

I could spend the rest of this book with examples like this.

The world of employee relations is fraught with conflicts, many of which are between the manager and/or supervisor and the people working for him or her. A myriad of laws govern this relationship. However, no law will stop the stupid manager and no law will erase prejudice, bigotry and chauvinism. It is important, then, to erase these elements from the workplace, which can and will lead to legal violations.

Managers can avoid employee problems by following one basic concept: "Treat your employees as you would wish to be treated in a similar context." What I mean by context is that you need to place yourself in the other's shoes, not just say, "Well if this were me, this is what I would want." For instance, if a lack of understanding as to why the other person was chosen for a position leads to resentment, a discrimination charge might be filed against you in an effort to find out why you made that decision. Defuse possible adverse situations by being "up front" with those you supervise and lead. Keep them informed about why decisions are made. Don't let the company newsletter or bulletin board give the affected employee the news. As the supervisor who made the decision, explain to all unsuccessful candidates why they were not selected. Encourage them to continue seeking advancement and other job enrichment opportunities.

My goal is to help you recognize potential conflicts, show you how to resolve them, and guide you in dealing with employee dissatisfaction, a discrimination charge or lawsuit. Because laws change and your individual situation is unique, no attempt has been made to cover every situation, nor should you consider this book "legal advice." For that, you should always consult your own attorney.

Further, this book is designed to provide you with basic information on the federal laws and case law dealing with employment. As you read through the book, remember that many states also have specific laws dealing with employment. If the state standards for a particular law exceed the federal standards, the state standard generally will apply. In some matters, conflicts have been recently resolved by courts so consultation with an employment law attorney would be wise. After reading this book, and before changing your policies, be sure to learn about your state's laws and the most recent case rulings.

PART ONE

DOING IT RIGHT

I have always felt that one manages processes and leads people. Therefore, although I do use the term "manager" throughout, I want you to think in terms of a leader or of leadership. Because as a leader of the people who report to you, you set the tone and you are responsible.

Once you have an understanding of goals and objectives, it becomes your job to put them into practice. This section gives you "hands on" advice as to what you can do to avoid equal employment opportunity problems.

It seems appropriate to begin this section with the first stage–recruiting your employees–and to end with terminating those who don't measure up.

RECRUITMENT

Once the employer is aware of position openings, it must consider by what method it should recruit candidates.

Word of Mouth

The courts and the Equal Employment Opportunity Commission (EEOC) have taken a hard position against an employer's recruiting practice that, although neutral on its face, perpetuates past discrimination. In light of this stance, an employer who recognizes that its employment makeup is substantially underrepresented by females or minorities would be ill-advised to recruit by word of mouth or nepotism.

Walk-In Applicants

When an employer is located in an area substantially lacking in minorities, he/she should not rely solely on this form of applicant flow.

Advertising

In situations as the foregoing, it is imperative the employer to seek other techniques of recruiting to acquire a broader selection of applicants. One such method is internet advertising. I suspect that 90% of job openings are now posted on-line. Most of the time you (the employer) never respond to the hundreds of applications you get on-line. However, if you are sued in a "failure to hire lawsuit," I recommend that you have these applications accessible. How can you defend against a charge of discrimination, if you don't have the documentation to prove that the successful applicant is the better candidate? Notice, I said *better* candidate, not the most qualified. You may choose someone with the minimum experience over someone with years in the field. The more experienced individual may have been a miserable person with whom you never want to work. Document this in detail and with concrete examples. Detailed documentation is the key to successfully defending a discrimination complaint.

Under Title VII of the Civil Rights Act and most state laws, an employer is prohibited from printing or publishing job notices or advertisements indicating any preference or limitation based on race, color, religion, sex or national origin, and some state laws include sexual preference, marital status, etc. Additionally, the Age Discrimination in Employment Act prohibits advertisements for jobs indicating preferences or limitations based on age for those over age 40. To avoid the risk of illegal advertising under these standards, the use of neutral job titles such as salesperson for salesman should be considered. If non-neutral job titles are not possible, the designation Equal Opportunity Employer M/F, prominently defined in the ad as meaning men or women, should follow each job listing. The Age Discrimination in Employment Act and Title VII make advertisements tending to discriminate against persons in a protected age classification unlawful. The following specifications in advertisements have been held to be unlawful both under Title VII and the Age Discrimination in Employment Act:

A. Male (or female) help wanted (stated alone)
B. Salesman (use neutral title of salesperson)
C. Pressman, Girl Friday wanted

D. Waitress, Janitor or Janitress (each alone)
E. Waiter (without M/F)
F. Stewardess, Attractive Female Desired
G. Use of sex-oriented column in newspaper
H. Single only (marital status is prohibited from use in many states, *e.g.*, New Jersey, New York, Nebraska)
I. Woman to work in office
J. Bright, young marketing representative
K. Age 25-35
L. Young
M. Boy
N. Girl
O. College Student
P. Recent College Graduate
Q. Age 40-58
R. Age over 50
S. Age over 65
T. Retired person
U. Supplement your pension

In contrast, the following have been determined to be lawful under the Age Discrimination in Employment Act and Title VII:

A. College Graduate
B. Not under 18
C. Not under 21
D. Flight Attendant
E. Machine Operator
F. Energetic Marketing Representative

It is important to distinguish jobs which do in fact require gender-based advertising, for instance, a male washroom attendant for a men's room. There are few of these jobs, but if you have one, it is legal to advertise by gender.

Minority Recruitment Services

Employers who are located in an area with few minorities would be well advised to consider the use of minority recruitment sources. Where no such local recruitment source exists, the employer should seek candidates from the state job service. When seeking candidates for labor positions, the scope of the recruitment area is typically held to be the surrounding area or, at most, the county and its surrounding area. When recruiting for management positions, the EEOC generally considers affirmative recruiting to be nationally or at least regionally conducted.

Maintaining Copies of Advertisements

As a general policy, a copy of all advertisements for each opening should be kept on file for at least one year after the opening is filled.

Applicant Flow Chart

This device enables the employer to maintain a record of the applicant pool from which the employer is able to recruit. The form should be completed by someone other than an individual in the hiring process, e.g., receptionist. This information is particularly significant in refuting potential applicant flow statistics where the charging party is seeking to demonstrate that the company fails to hire minorities/females for various positions. By the use of this form, the employer can identify the exact number of applicants by race and sex specifically seeking the particular position in question rather than having to rely on either all applicants applying irrespective of position sought or the potential applicant flow.

Recommended Recruiting and Hiring Procedures

The following 12 pointers have been extracted from various cases regarding subjective criteria in employment decisions and, if utilized, should help negate a challenge against the use of subjective criteria in hiring and other employment decisions.

1. A determination should be made of the necessary traits that are necessary for successful performance of the essential functions of each position. Thus, a job analysis should be developed to discover the necessary competence level or work behavior which the subjective criteria are designed to detect. It is critical to define the "essential functions" of the job. It is highly suspect, for instance, if you have a long list of experience required for an entry level position for instance.

2. The interviewers should be given precise written guidelines on those abilities and skills for which they are searching–again in line with the essential functions.

3. If experience is necessary, it should be achievable through any means and not limited to one specific area. In other words, an employer <u>must not</u> equate leadership exclusively with military service <u>but not</u> with teaching school, since this has been found to be sex discrimination. Certain kinds of experience common to one group only should <u>not</u> be the sole means by which an applicant can establish that he or she deserves to be hired or promoted.

4. The factors indicative of the necessary competence to fill a job should not be unduly vague.

5. The evaluative process should be uniform and call for discreet judgments. Some courts have held: "given the wide discretion that interviewers and supervisors have to measure the 'total person' and to waive criteria if other criteria are satisfied, it is possible that, at least in some cases, the criteria have been applied more stringently with regard to women."

6. The necessary factors for successful selection should have assigned weights. The weights must be defensible in terms of their relationship to job performance. In the absence of such weights, comparative judgments between candidates with different skills become subject to the whim of the interviewers.

7. The interviewers should act on the basis of first-hand knowledge.

8. Safeguards should be instituted against the intrusion of bias, such as an establishment of an appeals or review committee for minorities who have been refused hiring or promotional opportunities.

9. Vacancies ought to be announced internally so that all interested employees can have the opportunity to apply. Alternatively, companies should provide pre-registration of interest under which an employee is automatically considered when a vacancy arises.

10. Initiation of the bid for promotion or transfer should lie with the employee, not the supervisor, maximizing the possibility of indications of interest. Limiting employees considered to those tapped by supervisors perpetuates the likelihood of White male bias (when a majority of the supervisor are White males).

11. Finally, before recruitment can be successful, the supervisor should be able to answer at least the following questions:

- What does the current employee do?
- Will those duties change when the current employee leaves?
- Will the employee determine the duties?
- How does the current employee do the job?
- What is the end product or objective of the job?
- What qualifications does the person in the job need?
- What single activity or group of activities does this person spend most of the time doing?
- How often is this person supervised?
- How closely will this person be supervised?
- Is there a rule book to follow?
- With what types of people does the manger interact?
- How much pressure does the job entail?
- How much initiative is needed?
- How much creativity is needed?
- What character traits are necessary?
- What are practical possibilities for promotion?

- How much interference is there with normal family life?
- How much authority does the job involve?
- How much administrative know-how is necessary?
- What are the political aspects?
- What is the salary?

12. Never hire "by committee." It is fine to have others in the department meet a prospective candidate. However, the interviewer or supervisor must make the decision. Too often, the "committee" of peers wants to keep the status quo (e.g., no minorities), which will be discriminatory.

Do's for Advertising

1. **Do** list all positions in terms of neutral gender.
2. **Do** place advertisements in circulations that cover numerous areas or post on-line.
3. **Do** include the statement Equal Opportunity Employer Male/Female.
4. **Do** retain advertisements for at least one year from date position is filled.
5. **Do** limit the requirements of the job to those that are demonstrably job-related.
6. **Do** advertise in minority publications when statistics show the company is underutilized, but be certain that the publications are reputable.
7. **Do** include in advertisement a statement that the advertisement is for a particular position only.

Don'ts for Advertising

1. **Don't** advertise by gender.
2. **Don't** advertise by referring to age/sex/race.
3. **Don't** limit advertising to all-white localities.
4. **Don't** rely on word of mouth or nepotism when there is primarily an all-white workforce.
5. **Don't** maintain advertising when no openings exist (e.g., monthly rate holder ads, after a position has been filled).

6. **Don't** advertise in a paper or on-line resource that maintains male/female sections in employment.
7. **Don't** place educational requirements that are not job-related to a particular position.

HIRING

At a minimum, your recruitment procedures should be standardized, objective and centrally determined and reviewed. Ideally, one person should be charged with the responsibility of initially screening candidates for positions. When the supervisor in the area where the opening exists has final say over the hiring of a candidate, such supervisor should be made to identify specific deficiencies that resulted in the candidate's rejection. Although this should be the practice for all candidates, this rule should especially be followed when it involves the rejection of any person in a protected category (*i.e.*, pregnancy, women, applicants over 40, National Origin, etc.)

It is risky to allow individual department heads to publicize and determine how to recruit for specific job vacancies within their department. When they also decide <u>subjectively</u> whether an applicant's qualifications are satisfactory (without input from human resources professionals), the risk of exposure to a discrimination claim increases.

Never have applicants call just anyone in the company to find out if they have been hired. Always have a central contact person. Otherwise the applicant could get conflicting stories, which could inevitably lead to charges of unequal treatment.

Salary Administration

Your salary program (starting salaries, merit increases, promotional increases, etc.) should be applied equally to all affected employees. All rules, allowed percentage increases, etc. should be in writing so the supervisory personnel can administer the plan fairly and uniformly.

Regardless, whether or not you are a union employer, it is illegal under the National Labor Relations Act to prohibit your employees from discussing their wages with each other. **If this is in your handbook, take it out!**

The Act allows all employees to discuss wages, hours and working conditions.

The Interview

Hiring Standards

The key problem for an employer is that he/she must be prepared to demonstrate that the hiring standards do not automatically screen out minority or female applicants based on their speech, dress or work habits unless the hiring standards are demonstrably job-related. Perhaps the most important requirement is that hiring standards be fixed or reasonably objective. To that end, a job description detailing only the essential functions of the job must be a top priority.

Subjective hiring procedures which vest broad hiring discretion in department heads or individual supervisors give rise to an inference of discriminatory conduct. The following is a list of some of the more frequently encountered hiring criteria and the pitfalls, if any, connected with their use.

A. Police Records–Arrests and Convictions. Pre-employment inquiries into arrests and convictions are unlawful, absent a showing of business necessity. In April, 2012 The EEOC issued "Enforcement Guidance" on the consideration of Arrest and Conviction Records in employment decisions. First, the Guidance doesn't prohibit the use of arrest and conviction records. The

EEOC makes it clear that employers who treat applicants with similar criminal records differently violate Title VII. For instance, if a Hispanic applicant has a misdemeanor criminal record as does a White applicant, but you choose the White applicant, get ready to prove why the Hispanic applicant wasn't chosen. It had better not be based on the criminal records. Second, the EEOC cautions employers that if exclusions based on the criminal record disproportionately screen out minorities, the employer must prove that the exclusions are "job related and consistent with business necessity" under Title VII to escape liability.

B. <u>High School or College Requirement</u>. In the absence of a showing that the duties of the job which an applicant seeks require a high school education for successful performance, the requirement that the applicant possess a high school diploma is in violation of Title VII. The same may hold true for a college degree requirement. It has been held that a mere desire to upgrade the overall workforce quality by imposing such an education requirement or preference is not enough to justify such a requirement or preference in the face of a discrimination charge. Courts have held that this requirement disproportionally affects minorities.

C. <u>Hiring Standards that Discriminate against Women</u>. (No marriage rules, pregnancy, children.) A hiring standard that requires the exclusion of women because they are married when married male applicants for the same job are hired violates the sex discrimination provisions of both state and federal law. Similarly, it has been determined that a refusal to hire a woman solely because she is pregnant will also be found to violate the sex discrimination prohibition. Further, an employer may not, absent a showing that conflicting family obligations are demonstrably more relevant to job performance for a woman than a man, exclude women with preschool-age children from employment when no such restriction is applied to men. Also, the EEOC has ruled that a refusal to hire a woman solely because she is an unwed mother violates Title VII because (1) minorities as a group incur higher rates of illegitimacy than do Whites, and (2) there is no evidence that unwed fathers are similarly excluded from employment. Also, paying a newly hired female less than a newly hired male for the same job is a violation.

D. <u>Preference for Applicants Who Are Relatives</u>. Restricting hiring to relatives of current employees or of employees who have formerly been on the payroll can violate Title VII if minority groups are poorly represented in the existing workforce.

E. <u>Minimum Height and Weight Requirements</u>. Rigid adherence to minimum height and weight requirements often has a discriminatory effect against women, Asian, and Hispanic individuals. When such an effect can be shown, the standard will be held violative absent a showing that it falls within the bona fide occupational qualifications of Title VII and the state statutes.

F. <u>Rejection of Applicants Because of Poor Credit Ratings</u>. In the absence of business necessity, requiring employees to be good credit risks has been held discriminatory because minorities have poorer credit records in proportion to their representation in the population than do Whites.

G. <u>Hiring Standards Based on Age</u>. An employer may not refuse to hire an individual over the age of 40 because of his/her age unless age is a bona fide occupational qualification for the job. Nor can such a refusal to hire be justified by the requirements of any benefits or pension program. It is also unlawful for an employer to refuse to hire an older person solely because he/she receives Social Security benefits because such a policy discriminates against those within the protected age group. However, when a job applicant is unwilling to accept the number of scheduled hours requested by an employer because he/she does not desire to lose his/her Social Security benefits, the refusal to hire such an applicant will not constitute a violation of the Age Discrimination in Employment Act.

H. Hiring Standards Relating to Religion. Both federal and state laws prohibit an employer from refusing to hire an applicant because of his/her religion. In the event an individual is refused employment because of his/her religion, the burden is placed on the employer to show that the refusal to hire was a result of the inability to accommodate reasonably the employee's religious beliefs without undue hardship to the business. Undue hardship in this context has been defined as meaning the unavailability of any other employee to perform the job for which the applicant would otherwise be qualified during the term when the applicant was required to be absent for religious reasons. In January 2012 the United States Supreme Court ruled that religious institutions are not subject to various discrimination laws as applied to their ministerial employees (the Supreme Court did not specifically address lay employees). In that case the Hosanna-Tabor Evangelical Lutheran Church and School refused to accommodate a minister/teacher for narcolepsy. She threatened to file an ADA claim, and was terminated. The Supreme Court held that this was legal as the First Amendment right to freedom of religion prohibited the government from enforcing the ADA's requirements. Therefore, religious employers are not generally subject to discrimination laws as to their "called or religious" employees under the "ministerial exemption."

I. Hiring Standards Based on Citizenship. This is not an altogether clear requirement or absolutely established, but you should be cautioned that a refusal to hire based on citizenship alone may be contrary to the Civil Rights Act of 1866 and could also be a violation of the National Origin provisions of Title VII.

J. Hiring Standards Based on Performance Reports of other Employers. There is nothing unlawful in relying on a recommendation or performance report of an applicant's prior employer if the performance report or reference is itself not discriminatory or the result of prohibited discrimination. If the prior performance report is discriminatory, however, it has been held unlawful to rely on it as a basis for refusing to hire an applicant. Accordingly, in reference checking and obtaining reports from other employers, information must be considered with extreme caution, and every effort must be made to be objective concerning the applicant in view of the prior employer's comments.

Bona Fide Occupational Qualification: A bona fide occupational qualification (BFOQ) is basically that qualification absolutely necessary to do the job. Courts have held that employers must show that each hiring requirement is related (necessary) to doing the job.

Pre-Employment Inquiries

Although Title VII and most state laws do not expressly prohibit pre-employment inquiries concerning race, religion, sex, color or national origin, both the federal EEOC and most state commissions have taken the position that they will regard such inquiries with disfavor unless sex, religion or national origin is a bona fide occupational qualification or can be justified by a business necessity. Suffice it to say that rarely can an employer sufficiently prove business necessity. Employers will have to prove the question is relevant to the job. Additionally, certain questions, although not discriminatory on their face, will be regarded as evidence of a discriminatory purpose if the elicited information from which hiring decisions are made have a disproportionate impact upon minorities, females or others protected by discrimination laws.

Thus, for example, it has been held that inquiries into an applicant's arrest or conviction record are unlawful absent a showing of business necessity because certain minority groups experience higher rates of arrests and convictions. It has also been held discriminatory to require job applicants to produce an honorable discharge from the Armed Services because minorities receive a higher proportion of general and undesirable discharges. Using similar reasoning, the EEOC has determined that inquiring into a job applicant's financial condition discriminates against minorities since more nonWhites than Whites are below the poverty level. In this same vein, the EEOC has held that requesting an applicant to state the names of relatives employed by an employer may be evidence of discrimination if hiring preference is given to relatives of employees, and minorities are under-represented in the employer's workforce.

Under the Age Discrimination in Employment Act, it has been determined that inquiries into an applicant's age are not of themselves prohibited unless careful scrutiny shows that the inquiry indicates directly or indirectly a preference, limitation, specification or discrimination based on age. Similarly, it is not unlawful to require an applicant to state age or date of birth provided there is no discriminatory purpose in the question. Use of this inquiry is unwise since the EEOC views all inquiries on an application as the standards set by the company for employment.

Unacceptable Inquiries

The following are inquiries that should **not** appear on an application form or be asked during an interview.

Area	Unacceptable Inquiries
Address	Specific questions about foreign address, whether the applicant owns or rents home. Relationship of persons with whom applicant lives.
Age	Requirement that birth certificate or baptismal certificate be produced as proof of age. Questions concerning age on the application.
Ancestry	Inquiries into ancestry, mother tongue, national origin of parents or spouse.
Arrests	An inquiry relating to arrests unless a business necessity.
Birthplace	Birthplace of applicant or relatives. Requirement that birth certificate, baptismal record or naturalization papers be submitted prior to employment. Questions which identify customs or denomination. **After hire, employers may do so to satisfy the requirements of immigration laws.**

Childbearing	Questions on childbearing plans are discriminatory because they have an adverse impact on women.
Citizenship	Of what country are you a citizen? Are you naturalized or native born? Are your parents naturalized or native born? Requiring naturalization papers. **After hire, employers may do so to satisfy the requirements of immigration laws.**
Convictions, Court Records	To ask about or check arrest, conviction or court records if not substantially related to specific job functions.
Credit Rating	Any questions regarding credit.
Education	Questions about the nationality or religious affiliation of schools. How language skill was learned.
Handicaps	"Do you have any disabilities?" or questions which might divulge disabilities that do not relate to the job.
Marital Status	Inquiries about specific marital status, number of children; questions concerning pregnancy, birth control.
Military Record	Type of discharge.
Name	Inquiries about names which would indicate national origin. Inquiries about names which have been changed by court order, marriage or otherwise.
Organizations	List all organizations, clubs or societies to which you belong.
Photographs	Required prior to hiring.
Race	Applicant's race, color of skin, eyes or hair, height or weight where not relevant to the job.
References	Requiring religious references (except for a "ministerial" position)
Relatives	Name or address of any relative of an adult applicant.
Religion	Inquiry into religious affiliation, holiday observances, name of minister, etc. (except for ministerial position).

Sex (gender)	Sex of applicant. Inquiries which would indicate sex. Gender is not a bona fide occupational qualification (BFOQ) just because a job requires physical labor.
Hobbies	What are your hobbies, interests?

Acceptable Inquiries

The following are inquiries that **may** appear on the application or be asked in an interview.

Area	Acceptable Inquiries.
Address, length of residence	Applicant's address, place and length of current and previous resident. "How long in (city)?"
Age	If age is a legal requirement, "If hired, can you submit proof of age?" If applicant is a minor, proof of age in form of work permit or certificate of age.
Ancestry	Languages read, spoken or written.
Arrests	None (accept if truly a business necessity).
Birthplace	"Can you produce birth certificate or other proof of citizenship after employment?"
Citizenship	"Are you a citizen of the U.S.? If not, do you have the Legal right to remain permanently in the U.S.? Do you intend to remain permanently in the U.S.?" If hired, proof of citizenship may be required. Under the Immigration Control and Reform Act, you must get two forms of ID showing the person is legally in this country or one specific listed identification *i.e.*, passport.
Credit Rating	None.

Education	Academic, vocational or professional education; schools attended; language and office skills.
Emergency Contact	Name of person to contact in emergency.
Experience	Applicant's work experience; other countries visited.
Handicaps	"Do you have any physical, mental, or sensory disabilities which might affect the essential duties of the job you are seeking?" The applicant must know what the essential elements are or the question may be illegal.
Marital Status	You may only ask questions as to whether applicant can meet specific work schedules; any commitments which might hinder attendance. Anticipated duration on job or anticipation of absences if made to males and females both.
Miscellaneous	Notice that misstatements, omissions, false information on application may result in termination of employment.
Name	"Have you ever worked for this organization under another name? Is additional information concerning nicknames or change of name necessary to check work record or education? If yes, explain."
Organizations	Organizations, membership in which might relate to particular job.
Photograph	May be required after hiring.
Race	General distinguishing characteristics such as scars, etc.

References	Who referred you here? Areas of professional and character references.
Relatives	Names of relatives employed here. Names and addresses of parents of minor.
Religion	None, unless a bona fide occupational qualification.
Sex	Inquiry permissible only where bona fide occupational qualification exists. BFOQ's interpreted very narrowly by the courts.
Work Days	Choice of work days, shifts, where applicable.

The Three Goals of an Interview

In my opinion there are three goals in a job interview:

1. Tell the applicant generally about the job, specifically about the essential functions; describe the company and the work environment; and finally anything you feel is relevant that you think the applicant needs to know.

2. Draw the candidate out; get as much information about the person as possible. You need to find out if this applicant can and <u>will</u> perform the essential functions of the job. <u>This is your chance to listen twice as much as you speak.</u>

3. The most underrated function is that you need to leave a great impression of the company in the mind of each applicant. Let's face it. You may not get your first choice. So it behooves you to have every candidate wanting to work for you and the company. If you make them angry, belittle your boss or denigrate the company, you will never create a positive image, to your detriment.

Finding Out What You Need to Know

There are times when an employer must know whether or not the applicant can work late, travel, work weekends, etc. Whether the applicant has children or is married or has particular religious beliefs that prevent working certain days may be a legitimate concern.

What the interviewer may ask is whether the applicant can meet the requirements of the job, thus:

"We will need you to work every Saturday. Is that a problem?"

"We will need you to work until 7:00 p.m., three days a week. Is that a problem?"

This brings in the requirement at issue. If the applicant says "no problem" then the issue is closed. On the other hand, an employer would not need to hire that person if he or she said no. In other words, if the candidate can't meet the essential functions of the job for whatever reason (e.g., child care problems; no car, religious preferences–but be aware of the religious accommodation requirement), the law does not require the employer to hire that applicant.

Tests

Under the Equal Employment Opportunity Commission's Uniform Guidelines on Employee Selection Procedures, all standards established as a basis for employment are considered tests and, therefore, must be validated if there is disparate impact shown. These standards include tests other than the commonly recognized pencil and paper tests. The paper and pencil tests which supposedly measure general intelligence, aptitude, or personality traits considered to be relevant to the position have generally been found to be unlawful. They were found unlawful because, when analyzed, they were shown to affect minority groups disproportionately, and did not measure accurately whether the applicants could actually perform the job.

If the employer insists on standards (any tests or screening criteria) which create an adverse impact, whether or not neutral in their face, the employer will be required to have the standard validated.

To validate tests or standards found to create disparate impact requires costly and complex procedures involving psychologists who prepare statistical proof which determines the validity and reliability of the particular standards or tests in relation to the job they are designed to measure. Some tests, though, which are actual parts of the job, are lawful without validation. For instance, a secretary may be required to take a typing or grammar test, an engineer could be required to take an engineering test, and a welder could be required to take a welding test.

Once you have established valid testing criteria and procedures, do not allow department managers or supervisors to give their own tests when interviewing the candidates. These *"homegrown tests"* must be validated as well. But they rarely are. Supervisors sometimes feel they need to test special areas or skills. Do not allow this to happen, because it will lead to charges of disparate impact.

References

Reference checking is a critical step in the process of effective recruiting, but it may also be a source of discrimination litigation. To avoid difficulty, the employer should not seek information that could not be acquired through review of the application or elicited during the interview. In other words, only information that is job-related may be sought.

Information that is relevant to any position is the applicant's attendance and punctuality with his/her previous employer, the verification of his/her dates of employment, positions held and salary earned. Beyond these inquiries, questions asked may be susceptible to a charge of discrimination if the applicant is denied employment.

Employers should also avoid giving out any information over the telephone. If the decision is made to do so, care should be taken to give only the dates of employment and position held. Do not answer the question "Would you rehire?" because it may lead to a suit for damages by the employee who was denied employment. It has also been declared <u>illegal</u> <u>retaliation</u> for an employer to give a bad reference on a former employee because that employee brought an EEO charge or filed a lawsuit against the employer.

Hiring Husbands and Wives

Only where sound business reasons (business necessity) dictate may an employer refuse to hire (or retain after marriage) spouses. Generally, the courts have upheld policies which do not allow spouses to work in the same department, or have one spouse supervise the other. Elements of conflict of interest and lack of impartiality are often cited as valid business reasons.

However, when employees work in different departments and then marry, courts have held that a blanket policy requiring a spouse to resign is illegal. This is because most often the male employee has greater seniority, wages, benefits, etc. Therefore, the woman will terminate her employment. The courts feel this has a disparate impact on women and so have struck down the policy. However, if the employer can show that as many men as women resigned it may be able to avoid a disparate impact finding. Further, this may actually be "marital status" discrimination in some states. <u>Check your state laws, not all states protect marital status.</u>

The best rule to follow is that husbands and wives may work for a company, but not in any situation where one may supervise the other, or in the same department where it can be shown that a conflict of interest may develop.

Employment Physicals and
Pre-Employment Drug Screens

Physical examinations and drug screens as prerequisites to employment are legal provided the employer is able to demonstrate a legitimate, non-discriminatory business justification for the requirement. The need to justify the physical exam/drug test is not only important in the Title VII and Americans with

Disabilities Act settings, but is also important in view of the many state disability discrimination statutes in existence and the obligations of federal contractors and subcontractors under Executive Orders.

Promotions

It is illegal to apply standards for promotion differently to your employees. That means that all criteria you use in deciding who is to receive the promotion must be free of bias as to race, religion, color, sex, creed, disability, etc. You may not use subjective standards which have a disparate impact on protected groups.

In a significant court case, the court held the following practices unacceptable:

a. The foreman's recommendation was the key to promotion.

b. Foremen were not given any written instructions pertaining to qualifications necessary for promotion.

c. Standards which were the controlling factors were vague and subjective.

d. Hourly employees were not notified of promotion opportunities or the qualifications necessary to obtain the new position.

e. There were no safeguards established by the company to avoid discriminatory practices.

It is important that your promotion policies, although neutral sounding, do not discriminate.

Do's for Promotion

1. **Do** insist that the employee state the position or positions interested in, either by job bidding or during the performance evaluation.

2. **Do** conduct performance evaluations on all employees using written job specifications and standards to measure performance.

3. **Do** conduct evaluation meetings where employees both see the evaluation form and have an opportunity to sign it.
4. **Do** let employees know what is expected of them.
5. **Do** provide employees an opportunity to improve once they are put on notice that performance is below par.
6. **Do** maintain records of promotions by protected groups.
7. **Do** train supervisors to maintain an ongoing diary of their employees' work performance and behavior. This way, employees are not measured on the last good or bad event that the supervisor remembers.
8. **Do** maintain accurate attendance/tardy logs.
9. **Do** develop a system whereby promotion decisions are made by more than one person based upon specific factors of the job.
10. **Do** develop a system whereby employees may become aware of professional opportunities, as well as be afforded an opportunity to state their promotional interests.

Don'ts for Promotion

1. **Don't** make promotional decisions exclusively on the supervisor's visual observations and comments but utilize objective documented factors.
2. **Don't** make decisions regarding promotions without the employee's opportunity to bid or make the company aware of his/her interests.
3. **Don't** summarily dismiss an employee's interest in a promotional opportunity.
4. **Don't** tell employees that they would not be considered because of generalizations such as, "It's a man's job," or "It's too strenuous for a woman," or they would not like the environment because "It's male," or "It's White."
5. **Don't** preclude employees' advancement because of the lack of an educational level unless the educational requirements have been professionally validated to be "job-related."

6. **Don't** maintain the status quo if statistics reflect underutilization of minorities and females in higher level positions.
7. **Don't** make promotional decisions without input from employees on their particular interests. <u>There are few things worse than promoting someone who doesn't want to be a supervisor.</u>
8. **Don't** evaluate on subjective measures or generalities (e.g., attitude: use specific examples).
9. **Don't** allow one person to make promotional decisions.
10. **Don't** impose other "non-job related" barriers in promotional decisions (e.g., loss of seniority when going from one department to another).

Sample policies regarding promotion and transfer may be found in the Appendix.

THE PERFORMANCE APPRAISAL

One of the main reasons employers lose discrimination cases is because the performance appraisals of the employee in question are not accurate. In fact, supervisors who wish to be liked by everyone don't really do performance reviews. They simply write up all the good things they can think of, make the employee appear to "walk on water," give the standard rating, and let it go at that: in other words, a popularity report.

If your supervisors "falsify" performance appraisals in that fashion, you will have an extremely difficult time in proving that an unsatisfactory employee is not doing the job. Nothing is worse than a glowing appraisal dated a month before termination of the individual for unsatisfactory performance.

As an example, I represented a person I will call "Bill." He had been an underwriter for an insurance company for over 17 years, with "walk on water" annual evaluations. The company had a policy that before insuring any predominantly or all wooden structure, the underwriter had to make a personal visual inspection of the property. Bill only looked at a digital image, never left his office and wrote the insurance for $100,000. The building burned to the ground, a total loss. Bill was fired. At a jury trial for his wrongful termination, the company tried to show that Bill was fired for a progression of poor underwriting decisions, and this was the last straw.

However, they had no documentation and the supervisor had to admit that the evaluations, <u>done on company forms</u> were the only documents concerning Bill's performance. Recall, these were all glowing. Yet incredibly, the supervisor tried to persuade the jury that they really didn't reflect Bill's performance. He testified that he rated Bill higher to "motivate" him to do a better job. So on cross-examination I asked a simple question, "So you falsified a company document, didn't you?" To which he had to answer yes. We obtained a significant jury award.

The lesson is that you simply cannot "dummy up" an evaluation form. As I go around the country lecturing on this topic, I find that because people hate confrontation, they don't give accurate performance evaluations. <u>Get over it!</u> You are the boss. Be honest and candid in your assessment. Otherwise you could be setting the company up for a big lawsuit.

A few principles to remember:

a. A performance review accurately reflects the employee's actual performance during the period under review (e.g., six months, a year, etc.).
b. The performance appraisal in most companies is tied to salary merit increases. <u>But money should not become a motivator</u>. It rarely works. ("They still don't pay me enough for doing this lousy job with an even worse supervisor.")
c. The performance appraisal is used as a tool in setting goals and those elements necessary for the employee to retain his or her job.

The performance appraisal is not:

a. A motivation tool (*e.g.*, "If I give her a good evaluation, she will perform better.")
b. A device to obtain the approval of subordinates.
c. A way to give undeserved salary increases.

A supervisor has the responsibility to evaluate employees honestly. If that means "telling it like it is," then by all means do so. If there is nothing good to say, then that employee should be terminated. <u>Companies often make the mistake of not firing people who should be fired</u>. Then when a new supervisor applies standards correctly, the employee screams discrimination. And you as a company have allowed the poor behavior, which you now have to backtrack and justify.

Let's back up a minute, however. If there is nothing good to say to the employee, I hope that the appraisal interview was not the first time the employee heard the negative criticism. After all, it seems that if supervisors are doing a good job of managing (leading), they should have brought the employee's deficiencies to light long before the annual appraisal interview. The appraisal should not be a surprise and a weapon of psychological warfare between the supervisor and the employee.

And another thing: Was the employee told what was expected on the job? It seems rather inconsistent to point out deficiencies if the standards by which the employee must live have never been set. Tell all your employees what is expected of them, so that they can't complain that "you never told me!" Some courts have found in favor of terminated employees who were never told of the job rules! And that is doubly true for unemployment compensation claims by terminated employees.

Keep Notes

If your company uses annual appraisals and ties them to salary merit increases, supervisors must be accurate in what they are doing. Can a supervisor remember what an employee did that was good or bad two months ago? Five months? Ten months? Of course not! When many employees are supervised by one person, the task of remembering the performance of each one over a year's time is Herculean and next to impossible. <u>Only stupid managers rely on memory instead of documentation!</u>

Therefore, keep a separate sheet of paper, or an electronic record (or better yet a company form designed for this purpose) for each employee and occasionally note on it the good and bad things the employee has done and the date. This is not to intentionally build a case against an employee. It is simply a device to remember the highlights of each employee's performance. If done accurately, consistently, without bias and for every employee, the process is legal.

At appraisal time the supervisor accesses the notes and accurately charts the employee's job performance.

Playing Favorites

Of all management/leadership decisions, playing favorites is the worst (except maybe disciplining employees in front of their peers). When it comes to the performance appraisal (as in the employee selection procedure), we tend to follow the rule that "likes prefer likes." We all associate with and like people who have similar interests, backgrounds, and customs. However, real leaders put aside their personal prejudices and review performance only–not personal characteristics that they regard as offensive or objectionable (*i.e.*, long hair, piercings, sexual preference, pregnant employees, etc). Non-job-related factors should never enter into the appraisal of the employee's job performance.

Even though supervisors may not like the person, they are still obligated to treat all employees fairly and evaluate them on their actual job performance. The checklist provided should be reviewed prior to going into the appraisal interview regardless of what system you may be using.

Elements of an Employee Performance Appraisal System

Uniformity is the key word for employers. In a small operation, it is not as hard to make sure supervisors are using the same standards. In larger companies it is extremely difficult to obtain uniformity and consistency among supervisors in totally different areas (*i.e.*, accounting, manufacturing, sales, etc.) or shifts (day and night shift supervisors for example).

It is therefore extremely important that some type of monitoring or audit procedure be implemented. Employers want consistency because employees will charge that one employee is receiving preferential treatment or better performance reviews. The differences may have nothing to do with either of the employees, but with the appraisal methods used by the two supervisors using the same form. It is difficult to justify differences when there is no basis in fact for them. Supervisors should be trained in how to evaluate their employees against a common standard used by the entire company.

As an example, I represented a company in a sex discrimination case where one manager's idea of tardy was one minute past start time. Another felt that as long as the employee completed the job assignments, he didn't care when they came in. Both of these employees, one male, the other female were non-exempt. The female was fired for attendance issues, and the male was not. She compared herself to the male who, under a different supervisor was consistently "late" with no repercussions. There was no business necessity defense. It was a different management philosophy between the two supervisors, although the company preached that clocking in on time was the gold standard. We settled that case.

Here, then, are some guidelines which should be followed when setting up a new program or reviewing an existing one:

1. Evaluations should be based on the essential functions of the job established well in advance.
2. Appraisals should be in writing for all employees (or for those not in a labor organization where the contract controls) and should be signed by the employee.
3. If the employee refuses to sign, have a management employee witness that the appraisal form was given to the employee, and have that witness sign to so indicate.
4. Before a supervisor discusses his/her view with the employee, necessary approvals from upper management must be obtained. This avoids the awkwardness that

follows when upper management vetoes the decision of the immediate supervisor.

5. Supervisors must have available the employee's records on productivity and attendance where appropriate. Written data showing these elements of performance should be shown to the employee.

6. The company should have a program to audit supervisors. Many times these audits will reveal supervisors who consistently grade high and those who grade low (or the lazy ones that give everyone an average review). If it appears a supervisor grades all the employees "above average" or "outstanding," he or she should be counseled informally. Some companies put a limit on the number of "outstanding" grades one supervisor may give. A rule of thumb used is 10 percent outstanding, 10 percent below average and the rest of the categories in between. If salaries are tied to the appraisal system, this limit will keep salaries uniform among departments. The problem with this system is that if you tell your employees that great performance will yield great rewards and then impose limits, pretty soon your work force will catch on and most will level off because they see no reward in going the extra mile.

7. Often when the salary plan is tied to the performance appraisal system, supervisors will give inflated appraisals so that certain employees get more money. An audit will reveal this and prevent assessments that are out of line with the actual performances.

8. If an employee is rated marginal or unsatisfactory, but is to be retained, formal goals and objectives must be developed between the supervisor and the employee.

If your organization is not satisfied with the form it is currently using, several companies produce them. Many times the local office supply company will have them. Look for a form which clearly has objective criteria as its base.

The performance appraisal the supervisor fills out today can be the difference between winning and losing a charge of discrimination or lawsuit tomorrow.

Supervisor's Checklist for a Performance Appraisal Interview

A. <u>Preparing for the Interview</u>

- Determine beforehand what you are going to say in the interview.
- Decide on your major goal for the interview.
- Determine the most important matters to be considered, and steer the discussion to revolve around those points.

There should be no more than three major points. The rest can be covered generally.

B. <u>Time</u>

- Give the employee advance notice of the time of the interview. Give the employee a copy of the completed form in advance so he or she may review it beforehand. The interview should not be the first time the employee has seen the appraisal.
- Arrange for a quiet location.
- Be sure that you have privacy and try to avoid interruption.

C. <u>Conducting the Interview</u>

- Briefly discuss topics of general interest to establish a rapport with the employee.
- Discuss all aspects of the job; go over each area of accountability separately. Although you must point out both strengths and weaknesses, it will probably be more effective to discuss positive aspects of performance first.

- Try to avoid appraisals that are completely negative. If this cannot be avoided, termination must be considered as an alternative.
- Focus on performance rather than personality.
- Be constructive rather than destructive. If there are weaknesses, point them out but emphasize what can be done to rectify the situation. Do not attack the employee personally.
- Discuss advancement possibilities and what the employee can do to move upward. Be careful, however, not to make promises that cannot be kept. Any promises you make should have been confirmed by upper management, if necessary. Solicit any questions or complaints or comments that the employee may have.

D. Concluding the Interview

- Briefly review the important points of the appraisal.
- Carefully restate the details of any proposed courses of action that you have recommended.
- Be sure that the employee has had sufficient opportunity to say everything that he/she intended.
- At the end of the interview, allow the employee to fill out the employee comments section.
- The form must be signed by the employee to verify that he/she has read it (not necessarily that he/she agreed with it).

E. After the Interview: Your job is far from over!

- Periodically check the employee's activities to determine whether or not goals discussed at the interview are being attained.
- Offer assistance in achieving objectives.

DISCIPLINE AND THE DISCIPLINARY INTERVIEW

Discipline in its most negative sense means punishment and in its most positive sense means corrective action. My philosophy is that good, effective leaders don't "punish" their employees. They seek to correct the employee's performance and motivate them to change so that ultimately, the employee will not be terminated. The manner in which the supervisor perceives the action and thus carries out its performance will ultimately affect the outcome. For this reason, it is extremely important that every supervisor consider discipline as a means to modify behavior rather than to punish an indiscretion. Be creative; use this session to motivate an employee to do a better job for you.

To this end, the supervisor should remember the following guidelines:

- An employee is a person with emotions.
- No person likes to be belittled or chastised.
- Employees should be able to leave the disciplinary interview with self-respect.

- A supervisor should explain the purpose of the disciplinary report is to correct the employee's indiscretion/performance so similar conduct will not ensue. The report is not to be considered punishment.
- A supervisor should never discipline an employee in front of his/her peers.
- A supervisor should never engage in a shouting match with the employee, but should terminate the encounter and meet with the employee at a later date.
- A supervisor should always provide ample opportunity for the employee to offer his/her side of the story.
- A supervisor should allow the employee to document objections and attach them to the statement.
- A supervisor should seek the signature of the employee to indicate that the meeting was conducted and the employee received a copy.

Violations of policies should be grouped in various categories so that they carry different penalties. For instance, excessive absences and tardiness can be put together; violation of work rules such as drinking, stealing, fighting, swearing, etc. can be combined with those infractions receiving the same punishment.

Investigate

When it comes to discipline, the supervisor must make a concerted effort to find out all the facts before administering corrective action. The goal is to modify behavior and salvage a good employee. Again, it is not to punish. Therefore, the supervisor, in order to be fair, must investigate thoroughly. This means not only discussing the incident with other employees if appropriate, but also getting an explanation from the employee.

If the offense is extremely serious (such as stealing or sexual harassment), it is appropriate to suspend an employee for a time until the investigation is completed. This should not be longer than five working days. If the employee is exonerated or otherwise comes back to work, the time off should be considered compensable time off with pay given to the employee. If the employee is found guilty, the termination date is that date the employee was suspended. Your analysis prior to the disciplinary interview must include the seriousness of the offense. Separate the company violations into serious and minor offenses and act accordingly.

How Long Should Prior Discipline Remain Active?

There is no definitive time period for which to actively maintain disciplinary reports. Common sense and some arbitration and EEOC cases seem to indicate that discharge should not ensue for cumulative violations that extend for several years. The theory is that past violations remote in time do not shed a proper light on the employee's current behavior. Therefore, it is recommended that no disciplinary action be considered or kept in the employee's file for longer than two years. Whatever time frame is utilized, it is essential that it is used consistently for all employees.

Do's Regarding Discipline/Discharge

1. **Do** maintain specific written work rules.
2. **Do** communicate such rules either by handbook or intranet, posted work rules or, preferably, all those.
3. **Do** develop progressive discipline except for certain listed serious violations.
4. **Do** maintain a log of all discipline administered to be kept by a central person in most cases the human resource professional.
5. **Do** insist that before any disciplinary action is taken, the person maintaining the log is contacted to be certain that discipline is consistent throughout the facility.
6. **Do** discipline when the violation occurs or within a reasonable time to allow for investigation.
7. **Do** investigate thoroughly before taking disciplinary action by interviewing all participants and witnesses and taking statements whenever possible.

8. **Do**, where a union is involved, provide the employee an opportunity to have a steward present if one is requested for investigative interviews.
9. **Do** always inform the employee the purpose of discipline is not to punish but to correct.
10. **Do** progressive employee disciplining for same or similar conduct (insubordination, fighting – correct; insubordination, attendance – incorrect).
11. **Do** maintain all disciplinary write-ups for at least two years.[1]
12. **Do**, when writing a disciplinary action, state the likely action for future violations.

Don'ts Regarding Discipline/Discharge

1. **Don't** verbally discipline without documenting and placing in file.
2. **Don't** place any disciplinary slips in a file without getting the employee's signature on them or at least a witness who will attest to the fact that the discipline was received by the individual.
3. **Don't** apply different disciplinary action for similar conduct.
4. **Don't** discipline or discharge without a thorough investigation.
5. **Don't** discipline or discharge without thorough documentation.
6. **Don't** discipline or discharge without first allowing the person being disciplined or discharged an opportunity to explain his/her position.
7. **Don't** discipline or discharge where the employee is not aware of the rule violated because the employer failed to communicate it.
8. **Don't** accumulate violations for the purpose of making a case against an employee.

---

[1]   I recommend at least two years, but no retention period has been legally established.

9. **Don't** consider the employee's protected status (*i.e.*, pregnancy, age, gender, National Origin, race, etc) when determining discharge.
10. **Don't** overlook work rule violations of the supervisor's buddies.
11. **Don't** ignore minor violations intending to wait until several minor violations occur before writing up employee.
12. **Don't** try to remember employee violations; write them down.
13. **Don't** discharge employee for minor violations unless employee has been progressively disciplined for same or similar occurrences.
14. **Don't** maintain disciplinary write-ups for period greater than two years.[2]

Progressive Discipline

Progressive discipline is important in that it allows you to correct employees' workplace conduct and performance and cuts down on turnover. The idea is that you will maintain discipline (corrective action) at progressively harsher levels until the employee either changes or is terminated.

A key to good employee relations is firm and fair discipline, uniformly administered. A progressive system is helpful in maintaining uniformity. <u>However, you should always state that steps may be skipped depending on the seriousness of the violation. If you wish, you may design a system that works for your company.</u>

Typical Steps.

VERBAL/WRITTEN. Counsel with employee regarding indiscretion and indicate that informal statement will be placed in employee file regarding meeting. Inform that if no further violation ensues within a year, the letter will be removed.

---

[2] I recommend at least two years, but no retention period has been legally established.

WRITTEN WARNING. A second violation for the same or similar offense. Detail the violation in writing; be specific about date, time, event. Refer to earlier warning giving date. Inform of the consequences if the same or similar situation occurs again.

THREE-DAY LAYOFF WITHOUT PAY. A third violation for the same or similar offense. Detail the violation in writing. Refer to previous verbal and written warning by date. Inform of the consequences if the same or similar event occurs again.

DISCHARGE. A fourth violation for the same or similar offense. Detail the violation in writing. Refer to previous warning by date. Explain that employee has been given more than adequate opportunity to correct improper behavior, but that the company can no longer tolerate it.

TERMINATION

My philosophy is that employees terminate themselves. If you have done your job in providing constructive feedback and progressive discipline, and the employee still doesn't get it, terminate them. Another of my "words to live by" is that employers don't fire people soon enough. After giving the proper corrective action and counseling, what more can you do? If you ignore the problem, then you set an example for the other team members. At some point, you have let it go on so long, that it becomes almost impossible to terminate someone. This becomes especially an issue for a new supervisor trying to repair the damage done by the former boss.

How many managers really like to terminate an employee? Often a manager who has to terminate another individual becomes extremely apprehensive and, because of this anxiety, can make major mistakes in how the termination is communicated to the terminated employee. No employee should be terminated by a supervisor alone. There should always be either a human resource person or another management line witness. This to protect against the "he said/she said" scenario.

There is a proper way of terminating a person so that the degree of anxiety connected with the termination is held to a minimum. In my practice I see the evidence of "harsh" terminations. Either I get an employee who wants to sue the pants off the employer, or I get a call from the employer to defend a wrongful termination case because of the manner in which the supervisor fired the employee. Therefore, I find the ideas below helpful.

Some suggested approaches are as follows:

1. Terminations should occur on Mondays or Tuesdays, never on a Friday at 5:00 P.M. I have never figured out why supervisors wait until Friday at 5:00. People, once you have made the decision, why are you waiting? My experience is that the employee knows they are about to be fired. This is because (hopefully) you have done the right thing and let them know over time their performance deficiencies. So why wait? They can do damage to your computer system by leaving them in the job, among other things. Once you have made up your mind, terminate the employee. <u>One of the worst things a supervisor can do is not fire people who should be fired. Make sure you have the documentation!</u>

2. The actual act of termination should occur within the first 10 minutes of the termination interview. This is because the remainder of the time during the interview should be spent allowing the individual to express his or her hurt and, in essence, question why the termination occurred. And even then this time should be short as well.

3. Managers who do terminations should never be defensive and feel they must argue or persuade the individual that the termination is justified. This is a fruitless exercise, since once an individual realizes he or she is being terminated, he or she does not hear much else. A termination is never positive; individuals who are doing the termination should not try to make it a positive experience.

4. Managers should avoid platitudes and statements like: "I know how you feel," or "I am sure you will find another

job right away," and "You will find this a real blessing in disguise." Rather, managers should state the facts as they know them and try to give two or three good reasons why the individual was terminated. These reasons should not be debated or argued or even discussed in such a manner as to give the individual hope that he or she will be reinstated in the company.

5. Benefits afforded to the individual should be written out in a statement in an envelope to be handed to the individual at the time of termination. This is done because the individual may not remember what was said at the time of the termination and will find the written statement helpful to review at leisure.

6. Should an individual desire to see the manager who did the termination a day or two after the termination, the request may be granted depending on the circumstances. Sometimes it is good to have the terminating manager see the individual one more time to complete the process of venting and to sever the relationship with the company completely.

The most common errors in termination are:

a. Not firing the individual.
b. Firing in such a "hard-nosed fashion" that the individual is psychologically traumatized. Managers are encouraged to state the facts as they are and clearly communicate that the individual is terminated. It is not necessary to go into a personal attack and make statements such as: "You should have seen it coming," "You were not very bright," "You were not very talented," or "You are worst employee I've ever had" or any type of personal attack on the individual's skills or achievements. These are examples of comments from some of my actual cases.
c. Do not state that it is a "position elimination" or "staff reduction" unless it truly is one.

d. Managers doing the termination should stay away from any comments that show judgment on the individual's personal traits and/or habits. <u>Remember</u>: you don't want to strip the individual of his or her dignity.

e. Failure to have security present and make sure the employee is not allowed back on the work premises if you suspect the employee may become hostile and violent.

The above are in no way complete but are offered as suggestions for persons who must participate in the act of termination. The manner in which the termination is done may well dictate whether discrimination charges or a wrongful termination lawsuit will follow.

The Exit Interview

Some companies find it desirable to know why an employee voluntarily left the company and therefore conduct exit interviews. (Rarely would there be one when you terminate someone involuntarily). Exit interviews are conducted by someone in authority higher than the employee who is leaving, but not the employee's supervisor (*i.e.*, the office manager or HR). This promotes candor and preserves confidentiality. All exit interviews should be voluntary and strictly confidential. Only in that way can the company obtain a true picture of why the employee is leaving.

Here is one exit interview process:

An exit interview is a form of communication in which an employee who quit is given the opportunity to express fully or elaborate on his/her conception of the organization and its policies and his/her reasons for leaving. When conducted properly, an exit interview proves to be a great asset to any organization. The information gained from such an interview can be utilized to reduce turnover; upgrade the selection and placement process;

and to improve working conditions, unsatisfactory supervision, employee relations, and overall human resource practices. Legitimate suggestions and grievances uncovered during an exit interview can then be used as a basis for corrective action within the company.

The interview should be free-flowing, loose and not highly structured. This fosters better dialogue between the employee and the company representative. The goal is to have the employee volunteer information, rather than respond to yes or no questions only.

Once the information is obtained, the interviewer should make a confidential written report as soon after the interview as possible. Ideally this should be done immediately after the employee leaves. This will facilitate including the employee's direct quotes in the report.

Recognizing that each company will have its own goals in exit interviews, some general questions follow which you may wish to ask to get the ball rolling:

1. When hired, was your job clearly explained? Were its duties and responsibilities stated?
2. How would you describe the conditions where you worked while at the company? Were the working conditions, benefits, salary and hours clearly explained at the time of hiring?
3. Did you know at all times to whom you were to report? Did this person give easily understood instructions to you?
4. Did you feel a "sense of belonging" to the group with which you worked?
5. Did you feel that your job was worthwhile and meaningful?
6. When you needed assistance on your job, were you able to get it easily most of the time?
7. Could you discuss your job, suggestions for improving it, and your performance with your supervisor?
8. When did you first think about leaving the company and seeking other employment?

9. What was your job function at that time and did it contribute to this decision?
10. What is the real reason you are leaving the company? It could be because the employee was sexually harassed, but didn't want to file an internal complaint. This would be good to find out.
11. Could anything have been done to make you change your mind?
12. Do you have another job? How would you compare it with the one you are leaving?
13. Do you have any comments or general suggestions as to how we might make the company a better place to work?
14. Would you recommend our organization to friends or family as a place to work? If not, why not?
15. What type of training or reinforcement was available to you in your job?
16. In what ways did you not care for your job?
17. What can be done to improve communications between yourself and your fellow employees? With management?
18. Were you satisfied with the employee benefits provided you?

Notice the open-ended nature of the questions.

Finally, the report should go only to those managers and supervisors who can change company policies. It does no good to give this report to managers strictly for humorous reading. If you do, soon the interviews will become a joke to employees and managers alike.

Severance Agreements

Are severance agreements helpful, or do they put ideas in the minds of terminated employees? The employer must make that decision. However, in today's climate of ever-increasing litigation, it is safe to assume that employees already have a pretty good idea of the location of the courthouse or EEOC office.

> **NOTE**: EEOC regulations prohibit a provision in the agreement or a company policy that purports to prevent the employee from filing a charge of discrimination.

Form of Agreement

Depending on what is to be accomplished, the agreement can be a simple "voluntary" resignation, covenant not to sue, release or termination from employment. Many times, particularly in early retirement cases (The Older Worker Benefit Protection Act applies to agreements for people over 40) or potential discrimination cases, all of those elements will be included. Courts have held that a "voluntary" resignation in consideration of a good letter of reference was involuntary. However, the lawsuit was barred because the employee got the letter of reference in consideration of his leaving.

This often comes up in the context of telling an employee "quit or be fired." Supposedly, a voluntary termination looks better on the employee's record. Yet, we are all familiar with rulings by unemployment compensation tribunals that have granted benefits to someone in that position. They were "constructively discharged" and of course the termination wasn't truly voluntary.

These agreements can be used for almost all terminated employees to limit the employer's liability for unjust dismissal, age, sex, race, physical handicap, or any discrimination, or contract claims. **To be valid, something extra must be given other than the final paycheck due to the employee. This is what the courts term "consideration." It's something that the employer gives in addition to what is already owed.**

Contents and Validity of Agreement

Will the employee sign an agreement if he or she already harbors thoughts of suing his or her employer? Will the suggestion of an agreement lead the employee to believe that the employer has violated the law? These are considerations that should be reviewed by management and with counsel before a severance agreement is proposed. Further, you should check with legal counsel to make sure that the agreement is in line with state law.

What have the courts held to be lawful agreements? First, the employer must pay all sums that are due to the employee. Some states, such as California, New York, Nebraska and Arizona, have laws which provide for immediate payment of accrued wages upon the termination of the employee. Holding up the final paycheck in anticipation of getting a release may be against the law. Second, agreements must be "knowing" and "voluntary" and not signed under "duress." This means that if employees are forced to sign, it may be declared invalid. Courts have held that if the employee's attorney has reviewed it, the employee "knew." Some states have a presumption that if the employee signed it, he/she did so knowingly and voluntarily.

Also, in early-retirement cases, or in termination of senior executives, courts have held that they are more sophisticated and knowledgeable and so they entered into it "knowingly." Workers over 40 however, are covered under the Older Workers Benefit Protection Act and have certain rights. In those situations they have to be given notice that they can seek advice of a lawyer, can take up to 21 days to sign, and a have a 7 day rescission period (among other things) to be valid.

Both statutory (discrimination-type claims) and common law (tort, contract) causes of action have been held released as long as the release is knowing and voluntary. Therefore, both kinds of claims must be included in the agreement to avoid suits for unjust dismissal. This has been held invalid. But the release means the employee is not entitled to any damages. Some states also hold a release of unemployment claims invalid (*i.e.*, Arizona).

Employers should make sure that they are giving something extra that would not normally be granted to a terminated employee (cash, insurance policy, reference letter, stocks). This is the additional consideration necessary to the validity of the agreements.

Employers already engaged in discrimination suits or charges which then terminate an individual, must also obtain a release from the person for his or her attorneys' fees. Further, you can put in a non-disparagement clause if you think it is even remotely enforceable.

Finally, an agreement of confidentiality should be included to preclude newspaper coverage and other employees seeking similar terms. If the severance benefits are paid out over a period of time, they can be terminated if the employee breaches this clause.

Each termination must be treated separately. An attorney should review the agreement so that all avenues of the particular case are covered.

When properly drafted, severance agreements can eliminate potentially large liabilities.

Let me give you an example of a "stupid" (perhaps "careless" is a better word) manager. I represent a large client whose manager decided to find a severance agreement form on the internet. He filled in all the blanks and then sent it to the ex-employee. He then sent it to me for review. He had filled in the form to give the employee over 300 days of accrued leave. He meant "hours," but hadn't changed the form. The difference was about $90,000. Naturally the employee claimed that was the "negotiated deal." After defending the lawsuit, which we resolved short of trial, the client vowed never to use a fill-in-the blank form again. If you do use forms, please make sure you are filling in the blanks properly.

DRUG ABUSE AND ALCOHOLISM

In many states drug addiction and alcoholism are defined as physical impairments and illnesses which fall within Fair Employment Practices Acts. These conditions may also be covered under the Americans with Disabilities Act. States have made it illegal to discriminate against individuals so handicapped, and companies are required to make reasonable accommodations for those individuals. Naturally, if absenteeism is so high that the employee simply isn't there, management may terminate the person. No law requires an employer to keep an employee who can't do the work. The ADA provides that if a person is an active alcohol or drug user, that person is not a qualified person with a disability. However, if the employee is recovering you may need to consider a reasonable accommodation.

Supervisors must recognize that according to many state and federal laws, drug addiction and alcohol dependency are illnesses. Managers should treat these dependent employees the same as they would those who have other medical problems. If they are "recovering," then they are covered under the discrimination laws.

The policy should be that evidence of dependency alone should not be reason for dismissal. It is when the drug dependency or alcoholism results in repeated incidents of unsatisfactory job performance, excessive absenteeism, inability to carry out instructions or assigned duties, lack of cooperation, etc., that one must consider business necessity and reasonable accommodation. Business necessity may dictate that the person be removed from the job, transferred, suspended, etc. If a pattern of poor performance develops, the situation must be evaluated from both sides and with understanding of the employee's situation. However, the employee's lack of performance must be considered the strongest factor when a supervisor must terminate the person.

How does one find out or approach an individual where alcoholism or drug use is suspected? There is no blanket formula, as each person is different. Moreover, false accusations can only lead to trouble. Interview the employee in a private office and discuss his or her job performance. Indicate that there is a pattern of behavior developing. Ask the employee to explain it and why it is having a negative impact on his or her work. (Excessive absenteeism, insubordination, etc. may also be symptomatic of a divorce of which one is unaware or other family problems, e.g., unwed pregnant teenage daughter.)

Perhaps you will get a straight answer; often you won't. Experts on alcoholism report that treatment cannot begin until the person admits the problem to himself or herself. Therefore, he or she may not divulge it to a supervisor.

Managers must impress on the person, without mentioning the problem of alcohol or drugs that his or her job is on the line and that performance must improve. Set out the guidelines in writing and have the employee sign it.

<u>Remember</u>: Documentation is the key in those situations, as in all disciplinary actions.

If, on the other hand, there is direct evidence of drug or alcohol abuse or one has been made aware of it, the question should be discussed directly with the employee and he or she should be encouraged to seek help.

Recognizing that the average supervisor is untrained in detecting these problems, a list of characteristics (which is by no means exclusive) follows which has been generally accepted as indications of these illnesses.

Review these indications as ***possible*** presence of alcohol or drug dependency:

JOB PERFORMANCE	
Drug Dependency	**Alcoholism**
Absenteeism	Absenteeism
Lateness	Lateness
Unexplained absences from work area	Early departures
Frequent telephone calls	Long lunches
Frequent and lengthy visits to the restroom	Failure to meet work schedules
Frequent non-work related visits by strangers or employees from other areas	Occasional spasmodic work pace
	Decline in overall work quality or quantity

BEHAVIOR	
Drug Dependency	**Alcoholism**
Changes in Disposition	Smell of alcohol on breath (*Be careful! Some prescription drugs and other conditions may cause breath to smell like alcohol.*)
Frequent changes in mood and demeanor during the course of the workday	Changes in Disposition
Weight loss and poor appetite	Frequent changes in mood and demeanor during the course of the workday

BEHAVIOR	
Drug Dependency	**Alcoholism**
Excessive smoking	Weight loss and poor appetite
Bloodshot eyes dilated or constricted pupils, runny nose, irritation in both areas	Changes in personal relations with co-workers
Unsteady gait, trembling of hands and lips	Changes in grooming and dress
Slurred or rapid speech	Bloodshot eyes
	Occasional fights
	Slurred speech

Your company should also have a strong policy against the use of narcotics (drugs not prescribed by a licensed physician) and alcohol on company premises. If supervisors see such use, the employee should be terminated immediately. If supervisors hear of such use, they must investigate the incident thoroughly and only take action if they are certain of the truth. Also be aware if your state has a medical marijuana law. **Employees with medical marijuana cards may have certain rights. Check your state laws.**

Treatment and Referral

Let us assume there is a clear-cut case of alcoholism or drug addiction (or abuse). Every effort should be made to have the person seek help, even if the supervisor must terminate that person from employment. Most communities have local mental health or alcohol and drug abuse agencies. Refer the person there or any place known to treat these problems. And many insurance plans now provide coverage for alcohol and drug dependency treatment.

Drug Testing

Can you legally test your employees on a random, no probable cause basis? Do you need to have some probable cause? Are you violating employees' Constitutional rights? What is the difference between public and private employers in the ability to test? These are several questions plaguing both public and private employers today.

Unlike other policies and programs of human resource management, drug testing is a topic that is in constant flux. Many states have formal constitutional or statutory provisions governing it expressly, but no such federal regulations exist for private employers. The drug testing field is fairly wide open but becomes more regulated daily by challenges to testing programs brought under vague state and federal laws. State legislatures are increasingly supportive of drug testing bills which will create at least some guidelines for drug testing programs.

State laws must be reviewed to determine the elements of a drug testing program which will safely pass constitutional or legal muster.

Of course, an employer has a legitimate interest in the well-being of its business and its employees too. But when do those considerations collide with an employee's rights to privacy, free expression, due process, and freedom from unreasonable search and seizure? At least one court has suggested that the answer can only be found in a case by case "balancing test." For example, courts have found that some employees have a reduced expectation of privacy because of the sensitive, highly regulated or public nature of their work, e.g., bus drivers, jockeys, customs inspectors, etc. The employer's interest weighs more heavily in these "balancing test" cases, so broad testing programs have been upheld. However, broad testing programs have not been upheld for police officers and firefighters. Each employer-employee relationship must be examined on its own merits for "balancing test" purposes.

Case law indicates that in nearly every dispute over a drug testing program, the court will address two threshold issues: whether the employer is private or public (*i.e.*, the government), and whether the program calls for employee drug testing in a broad random fashion or simply for cause shown.

Even in "at will" states where a private employer usually may fire an employee for any cause or no cause, an employee cannot be fired for unlawful or discriminatory reasons. Government workers have substantial legal protection in their employment via federal and state constitutions. However, because federal and state constitutions typically do not extend substantive protection of individual rights into a relationship between two private parties (the employer and employee) in their consensual dealings (the terms and conditions of the employment relationship), a private employer's drug testing program is much less likely to be attacked on a constitutional basis such as a violation of the employee's right to privacy. However, the private employers' programs may still be attacked if their state has statutes relating to a right to privacy. Some states such as California have applied the state constitution (privacy, etc.) to private employers. You should check with your lawyer to determine if your state constitution applies to private employers.

The second factor that courts will certainly address is the nature of the drug-testing program. Support is nearly unanimous for testing "for cause," that is, when an employee's actions tangibly demonstrate that he/she is under the influence of drugs or alcohol (for example, by his/her demeanor; or after an industrial accident). The other, more troublesome end of the testing program is random, or testing that is not "for cause," where the employee has given the employer no tangible reason to believe he/she is using drugs or alcohol. In order to survive a legal attack on a program like this, an employer is well advised to employ the most accurate test available. Follow the least intrusive testing procedures possible and have a system of securely storing and maintaining the employee test samples if you attempt to do your own testing. Every program should include breath, urine, blood, and hair testing. Moreover, no program should be without clear policies ensuring the utter confidentiality of employee test results. <u>Many states have laws which dictate the procedures you have to use.</u>

As a personnel policy matter, drug tests can be useful and helpful both to employees and employers in detecting and curing employees' chemical abuse problems. However, because the law in this area is shifting widely and frequently (not only among states but also between state and federal courts), employers are well advised to consult an attorney in structuring and implementing any drug testing program.

1. Public Employers

The United States Constitution and its Bill of Rights apply to the federal government, but also to state and local governments through the 14th Amendment. Thus, if there is "state action," employees can sue public employers for violation of their Constitutional rights under a federal statute, 42 USC §1983. Therefore, alleged violations of invasion of privacy, free speech, illegal search and seizure, denial of due process, etc. can be addressed in the federal courts.

The courts have generally held that if an employer has reasonable suspicion of drug use, testing may occur. There is now no longer any question that drug testing through blood, urine, or breath testing involves a search under the Fourth Amendment. Thus courts have used a "reasonableness" standard in the intrusion upon the person.

Since these Constitutional rights can be infringed upon by public employers, it is recommended that no random (without cause) drug testing be done, except in unusual or specific circumstances where the job requires that the employee be free from drug use or its effect. Another court upheld the U.S. Customs drug testing program, which conditioned transfer to sensitive jobs upon passing the test. There was a strong governmental interest in hiring people for key positions in drug enforcement. Courts have also upheld random drug tests in specific cases where safety was a factor, *i.e.*, nuclear power plant; prison guards in a penitentiary.

Moreover, public employers have the added burden, in many cases, of providing procedural due process to their employees. Thus firefighters were required to have due process protection in implementing a drug program, and random urinalysis violated their rights under the Fourth Amendment.

Since an exhaustive analysis of every situation is beyond the scope of this book, public employers, such as fire and police departments, schools, and county and city governments should definitely seek qualified legal counsel before implementing a drug testing program. Random drug testing absent statutory approval or business necessity is fraught with legal perils and should be examined closely.

2.   Private Employers

The U.S. Constitution does not apply to private employers unless they are engaging in "state action." Private employers will be held to be engaging in state action if their activities are so inter-twined in the government that their activities are fairly attribut-able to the state.

However, several state causes of action exist and have been held applicable to drug testing. Some common law (nonstatutory) causes of action are:

   a.   Defamation
   b.   Outrageous conduct
   c.   Invasion of privacy
   d.   Wrongful discharge

In addition, state constitutional provisions, state privacy stat-utes and other statutes may give an employee a cause of action. Many states are now adopting laws allowing employers to test for drugs, even on a random basis, as long as certain procedural guidelines and safeguards are met. For instance, Arizona and Nebraska have enacted such laws allowing mandatory testing (blood or breath) for drugs and alcohol. Certain procedural safe-guards are required (e.g., documentation of chain of custody of specimen required; preliminary screening must be confirmed by gas chromatography-mass spectrometry tests). The most onerous provision of the law for employees is that they may be fired for refusing to take the test–even if there is no reasonable cause. Many other states are passing similar laws and employers must be aware of what their individual state laws require (or allow).

Remember: Any random (no cause) test is subject to legal attack by innocent employees. Employers should check with legal counsel before implementing any drug testing program, as each state has specific requirements. Certainly, legal expertise must be obtained if a random drug testing program is contemplated.

3.   AIDS and Infectious Diseases

AIDS is considered a disability under the Americans with Disabilities Act. However, random blood screening has been held by several courts to be violative of the Fourth Amendment's prohibitions against illegal search and seizure in the public sector. A Federal Court held that mandatory blood screening for infectious disease (test was aimed at AIDS) was unconstitutional as violative of the Fourteenth Amendment. The Court engaged in an analysis of case law stating:

"To determine the appropriate standard of reasonableness... this Court must balance the nature and quality of the intrusion on the individual's Fourth Amendment interests against the importance of the governmental interests alleged to justify the intrusion."

The Court held that no amount of testing would control either the spread of AIDS, or curb the contraction of AIDS of the public employer. This case is significant for all employers because the Court recognized how AIDS is spread and felt that random blood screening did nothing to curb AIDS in the workplace.

In another public employer case, the court upheld an employee's motion to return to the classroom even though he had AIDS. The issue turned on Section 504 of the Rehabilitation Act, which applies to any employer receiving federal funds. (Similar provisions under the Americans with Disabilities Act apply to the private sector as well.) The issue was whether or not the employee was "otherwise qualified" as defined in the statute. The law states that no employer may discriminate against a handicapped worker as long as that employee is "otherwise qualified." The school argued that the employee was not qualified because of the potential risk he carried since he had AIDS. The Court rejected this and reinstated the employee.

A case brought under Section 504 and state anti-discrimination laws, was settled in favor of an AIDS-infected county employee. Terms of the settlement were $40,000 in back pay, $100,000 for medical expenses, $56,000 in attorneys' fees, reinstatement or a lump sum payment, if he was physically unable to go to work. Finally, the U.S. Supreme Court has held that a teacher with tuberculosis (an infectious disease) was covered under Section 504 of the Rehabilitation Act. This marked the first time the court had held this way and, of course, opened the door for AIDS victims and people with other infectious diseases to bring suit.

What all this means to employers is that employees with AIDS (and other infectious diseases) are protected by federal and state discrimination laws covering physical disabilities. Thus, employers must develop reasonable policies and guidelines when dealing with infectious diseases. Otherwise, they will be subject to lawsuits and charges of discrimination based on physical disability.

Policies should emphasize the privacy of the employee and also the safety of the general workforce, if such is at issue. When it becomes clear that the employee can no longer physically function in the job, employers are safe in removing that employee from the workforce. This is because they are then not "otherwise qualified." However, remember Section 504, the ADA, and several state laws require that "reasonable accommodations" must be made for the handicapped individual.

An employer who wishes to deal with infectious diseases must tread lightly and examine all aspects carefully. The rights of privacy of the individual are paramount. Mass hysteria has already done more damage to some individuals than the disease itself. Education and a reasonable approach will avoid many legal pitfalls that the overzealous employer could avoid.

Finally, employers should check state statutes. States such as Florida (CS/HB 1519) and West Virginia (HB 303) have enacted AIDS-testing legislation.

4.   Drug-Free Workplace

Several types of employers may be subject to *Drug-Free Workplace Act of 1988* (42 USC §701 et. seq.). The law requires federal contractors to provide a drug-free workplace in order to be considered a "responsible" source for securing certain contracts. These "covered" contracts are for property and services in excess of $25,000.

These employers are obligated to:

a. Publish a policy against use, possession, manufacture, etc. of illegal drugs and that those acts are prohibited in the workforce and that specific actions will be taken for violations.
b. Establish a drug awareness program informing employees of the damages of drug use.
c. Provide a copy of the policy to all employees.
d. Notify each employee that, as a condition of their employment, they must abide by the terms of the policy statement.
e. Provide sanctions or mandate satisfactory participation in rehabilitation program.

Each employer should also check with a knowledgeable attorney or a professional to determine the laws governing testing in its particular state.

Drug and AIDS testing is in a period of intense legal scrutiny. The individual's rights have been balanced against those of the reasonableness of the employer's interests. This balance has not always tipped in favor of the employer. In fact only truly legitimate business reasons have withstood the test of the court challenge. The law and court decisions are ever-changing. It is therefore impossible to give an exhaustive review of this area that wouldn't be by definition limited. The author has attempted to merely point out various areas of concern and highlight, where possible, the areas of real concern to both public and private employers.

Legal advice should always be obtained before any drug testing program is implemented. What is legal today, may be suspect tomorrow.

Remember: As with all medical conditions and physical disabilities, if the person absolutely cannot perform the requirements of the job, with or without accommodation, you may terminate that person. However, alcoholism and drug dependency should be treated with compassion as sicknesses even if termination is the only answer due to business necessity.

Tips For Leaders

In concluding this section, I want to share with you some of my thoughts on leadership which I have found helpful in training leaders.

1. Be honest with your employees and customers.
2. Inform your employees of what is expected and what is going on in the company. Knowledgeable employees don't fear change.
3. Along those same lines, empower your people to make decisions. Set the standards, parameters and goals, and then get out of the way.
4. Share your expertise. Give it freely so that you are building a team of high performers, not followers. This empowers people to move up the organization and builds morale.
5. Prevent turnover; many people think year one is the best year and it's all downhill from there. Keep motivating employees and take nothing for granted.
6. Know your company culture and the sub-culture in your department. Make sure everyone is on the same page.

7. Promote your company brand from within throughout the entire company. What can you do and what can't you do?
8. Set the standard for performance.
9. Use every opportunity to create teaching moments with you and your team.
10. Be able to laugh at yourself. Enter the workplace with a sense of humor. It will make you more likeable and the workplace more enjoyable for others.

There are countless other "tips." However, I find these to be a somewhat universal set that helps leaders become high achievers in their organizations.

PART TWO

EVALUATING WHAT
IS AT STAKE

This next section is the "why" of good equal employment practices. Following is a synopsis of each law affecting these practices, and discussion of them.

Moreover, this section provides information on selecting attorneys, how to deal with investigative agencies and discussions of legal concepts of alternative causes of action such as unjust dismissal.

Management would do well to understand the basic legalities and theories, so that it legally can adapt the human resource practices discussed in Part One to its own workplace.

One caveat: court cases or new legislation can change the interpretation of these laws. Every effort has been made to give current information. However, a major federal circuit court case or a Supreme Court decision could change or even expand the meaning of a statute.

ALWAYS check with legal counsel for the most current status of the law federally and in your state.

CAN YOU AFFORD IT?

A. Administrative Complaints

Complaints alone with little merit may be expensive because resolution means expenditure of time, legal fees and court costs.

Depending on how you view the matter, the filing of a charge of discrimination is a simple process. An injured party need not seek out an attorney in order to have his or her complaint investigated. The charging party has merely to present a complaint to a local Fair Employment Practice agency or the Equal Employment Opportunity Commission (EEOC) to start the investigation. At this point, the costs to the employer in time, effort, and legal fees begin to run. Even if the employer should prevail at some step along the way, the cost is significant. Therefore, the extra time taken to do things right, to document policies and administer them uniformly, is well worth the energy expended.

B. Jury Trials:

Title VII litigants are entitled to a jury trial.

C.   Types of Damages Allowable

BACK PAY: The vast majority of cases involving monetary remedies involve back pay. Back pay is the amount of money the employee lost in pay and benefits because of the employer's discriminatory acts. However, the employee cannot just wait for the "big check." Employees must take affirmative measures to reduce their back pay. In other words, they must seek out and accept (if offered), comparable work. I once represented a group of county officials in a sex discrimination case. The plaintiff had taken a job, but quit because she didn't like the work. The court, on our motion cut off her back pay to the date she quit. She was entitled to nothing further. As it turned out, it didn't matter because the jury ruled in the officials' favor. But the lesson is that employees must "mitigate" their back pay.

CLASS ACTION DAMAGES: In this type of case the employee, or a large group of employees, sue the company on behalf of all other employees (or applicants) who have the same legal and factual problems. The class action suit is the most costly to the employer. Further, based on its limited resources, the EEOC vigorously litigates these types of actions to uncover and eliminate the largest number of abusers. Class-wide actions result in substantial monetary recovery to those employees, prospective employees or ex-employees who are within the appropriate class. The back pay is magnified by the number of members in the class. As are the plaintiffs' attorneys' fees.

REINSTATEMENT/PROMOTION/SENIORITY: Depending on the type of discrimination, it is likely that as part of a settlement, consent degree or court decision, the employee(s) will be reinstated, promoted or granted seniority.

FRONT PAY: Should you be found guilty of firing someone illegally or denying someone a promotion for discriminatory reasons, the courts can and do award that person "front pay." Let's assume you have already promoted another individual but the court holds that you should have promoted the complainant. The court will not order you to terminate or demote the one you chose. Instead, you will immediately pay the complainant that salary he or she would have earned in the higher grade. Then when the next position opens up, you will then place that person in it. In the meantime, the employee will receive the higher pay, without actually being in the higher-rated position. Further, when reinstatement to the old job just won't work, courts will award partial pay instead of reinstatement.

COMPENSATORY DAMAGES: Under Title VII as amended in 1991, employees can now get money damages for emotional distress, pain and suffering, loss of enjoyment of life, inconvenience, and punitive damages. These will range from $50,000 to $300,000 (not including the back pay damages) per employee, depending on the size of the employer.

The cost in lost management prerogative and time is incalculable. The **hidden cost** of these matters is the countless hours your employees will spend on the defense of the case.

When the court takes away your right to hire and fire, you have lost the major management tool available: the right to hire whom you wish, when you wish. That is a "damage" that cannot be measured in dollars and cents alone.

The above is a brief statement of the potential costs and damages you may find imposed on your company.

D. Taxability

Tax issues are beyond the scope of this book. However, generally currently any amount recovered for whatever category of damages is taxable under federal law. This has had the effect of increasing settlements because employees want a net figure, not a gross amount, in order to settle a case. NEVER give your employees tax advice on the taxability of the settlement.

OVERVIEW OF THE LAWS REGULATING THE EMPLOYMENT RELATIONSHIP

Title VII of the Civil Rights Act of 1964

Whom It Covers:

All private employers of 15 or more persons;
All educational institutions, private and public;
State and local government;
Private and public employment agencies;
Labor unions with 15 or more members;
Joint labor-management committees for apprenticeship and training.

The Civil Rights Act of 1964 is comprised of 11 Sections called "Titles." Title VII of The Civil Rights Act of 1964 makes it unlawful for an employer to discriminate with respect to any condition of employment or against any applicant for employment because of race, color, sex, religion or national origin, except where religion, sex or national origin is a bona fide occupational qualification reasonably necessary to the conduct of a particular business.

The vast majority of employment discrimination suits are brought under Title VII and are often initially processed through a state Civil Rights Commission before actually being processed by the federal agency.

The EEOC (Equal Employment Opportunity Commission) was originally instituted in early 1965 to administer and enforce Title VII and other laws against workplace discrimination. Since that time, the EEOC has continued to be the agency in charge of administration and enforcement of numerous additional laws that have been enacted regarding workplace discrimination. Some of these laws are addressed in more detail below.

One of the implications of the administration and enforcement of the additional laws is that the EEOC has more vigorously prosecuted claims of discrimination. In addition, it has indicated that rather than concentrating on just large employers, it will also vigorously pursue claims of discrimination involving smaller employers. However, unless the claims have some bearing on the overall operation of the business (such as all females receive less pay than men), the EEOC has been reluctant to sue the employer on behalf of the employee, and instead issues the employee a "Right To Sue" letter. The employee then has 90 days in which to sue the employer in federal court. As stated earlier, jury trials are allowed in Title VII actions.

There is a major shift in the law to include as covered under Title VII, **transgender** discrimination. Several circuit courts have held that employers who discriminate against someone who changes their sexual identity violate the ban against discrimination "...because of sex." Eventually, the Supreme Court will weigh in on this. But for now when an employee comes to you and discloses that they are going to go from living as a man to living as a woman or vice versa, do not take adverse employment action against that person for that reason. Your stereotype of how you think a man or woman should act (*i.e.*, she's too masculine; he acts too much like a woman) has been held to be illegal sex discrimination when you take adverse action such as termination or rescission of a job offer.

However, as of this printing, sexual orientation is not covered under federal law. Look to your state or local laws for guidance on that. Some states make sexual orientation discrimination illegal. Title VII does not, nor has it been interpreted that way.

Most employees will get a Right To Sue letter and sue before the EEOC ever completes its investigation.

States have statutes prohibiting discrimination in employment. Most of these statutes cover sex, race, color, religion, and national origin. Some include marital status and sexual preference. Also many states have statutes prohibiting age discrimination. Some large cities, such as Philadelphia, St. Louis, and New York City, also have agencies established to combat employment discrimination.

Two Main Ways in Which Violations of Title VII May Be Identified: Disparate Impact and Disparate Treatment

In order to establish the bona fide existence of a Title VII violation, a *prima facie* case must be established. A *prima facie* case is one where the employee proves the minimum necessary to establish a violation of the law. For instance, in a sex discrimination case a woman must show that she is female; suffered an adverse employment action (or in a disparate impact case, that the policy at issue had a negative impact on females as a group); and that similarly situated males were treated differently (better).

A. Disparate Impact

Disparate impact usually results where a program or practice neutral on its face has a disproportionate impact on protected groups. To establish a violation under the disparate impact theory, the plaintiff must demonstrate that the program or policy at issue disproportionately (generally shown through statistical evidence) excludes more minorities than non-minorities, or women vs. men. If such disparities exist, then a *prima facie* case of discrimination is made out and no showing of bad faith or bad motive is necessary.

Examples of facially neutral requirements that may have a disparate impact:

1. A requirement that a worker be able to lift 100 pounds of weight.
2. A requirement that a worker be a least 5'6" tall.
3. A requirement that an applicant successfully complete a pre-employment aptitude test.
4. A requirement that a worker successfully complete a strength and agility test.
5. A requirement that an applicant weigh at least 150 pounds.
6. A requirement that persons arrested or convicted of crimes are automatically excluded from job openings.
7. A requirement that employees with an excessive number of garnishments be automatically discharged.

Under the disparate impact theory, the employee need not prove that the employer <u>intended</u> to discriminate, but merely that discrimination occurred.

B. <u>Disparate Treatment</u>

A *prima facie* case of disparate treatment is made by the plaintiff when it is established that a particular employment policy treats one employee differently than another. Or, more often, when a neutral employment practice is administered in an inconsistent fashion which results in a protected individual being adversely affected. As stated earlier, a *prima facie* case is the bare minimum that an employee has to prove before the burden shifts to the employer to come up with a legitimate business reason.

Examples of Disparate Treatment:

1. A non-White employee is fired for fighting on the job, whereas a White employee receives only a written warning.
2. A 50-year-old employee is laid off for having three unexcused absences in a six-month period, whereas a 25-year-old employee receives only a warning for the same offenses.
3. A White employee with three years experience is considered for a promotion to a foreman position, but the company waits until a non-White employee has five years experience before similar consideration is given.
4. A company offers stock options and fringe benefits to its male employees, but does not offer similar options to its female employees, since it assumes they are not heads of households.
5. All young, able-bodied workers are given a first choice of vacation days, leaving the remaining vacation days for older, disabled workers.

Federal Age Discrimination in Employment Act of 1967 (ADEA)

Whom It Covers

Employers of 20 or more employees including federal, state and local government, employment agencies, labor organizations, federal government and contractors (Executive Order 11141).

The ADEA makes it unlawful to discriminate on the basis of age against employees or applicants for employment who are at least 40 years of age. It is similar to Title VII in that it prohibits a wide range of conduct where such conduct is based on age, as it affects those over 40 years of age. The "Age Act" is administered by the EEOC. Further, if you have been found guilty under this law, you may be assessed the amount of the actual damages, plus the same amount as a "punitive" award for a willful violation. Either party may have a jury trial under this law. Effective January 1, 1985, employees are required to notify employees' spouses who reach age 65 that they may continue their present health insurance or use Medicare. No longer may employers reduce employees' spouses' benefits who reach age 65.

Sixty days after the charge is filed, an employee may sue the employer in federal court. No Right To Sue letter is necessary.

Executive Orders

Employers who are contractors or subcontractors of the federal government must adhere to the terms of certain Executive Orders as a condition of their contracts. These obligations are in addition to those imposed on all employers by other laws relating to discrimination.

The key regarding the applicability of the Executive Orders is that the employer has a government contract. It bears emphasis, however, that the term "contract" is broadly construed. Thus, even if a contract does not specifically refer to one of the Executive Orders, you must comply, unless exempted, simply by virtue of your status as a government contractor or a subcontractor of a business which contracts with the federal government.

Executive Order 11246

Whom It Covers

Contractors and subcontractors who have a contract or contracts with the government totaling $10,000 or more during any particular year; all government contractors and subcontractors with 50 or more employees and contract or contracts of $50,000 or more must also develop a written Affirmative Action Program.

The heart of this Executive Order is the responsibility placed on the contractor to accept and implement the "Equal Opportunity

Clause." This clause requires the contractor or subcontractor to:

- refrain from discriminating against any employee or applicant on the basis of race, color, religion, sex, or national origin;
- take affirmative action to insure that all employees and applicants are treated without regard to race, color, religion, sex, or national origin;
- comply with all rules and regulations promulgated by the Secretary of Labor pursuant to the Executive Order.

Not only is the employer obligated to comply with the Equal Opportunity Clause, but it, in turn, must require any subcontractors to adhere to the obligations of the Equal Opportunity Clause.

By virtue of its status as a government contractor, the employer may be subject to investigation by the contracting agency or the Secretary of Labor. Sanctions can be imposed for non-compliance up to and including suspension of its right to bid on government contracts, debarment, or publication of non-compliance. Monies due under certain contracts may also be withheld. The Office of Federal Contract Compliance Programs (OFCCP) administers these Executive Orders.

Executive Order 11758

Whom It Covers

All contractors or subcontractors who have a direct federal contract with the government for $2,500 in any particular year are covered.

This operates in a manner similar to that of 11246 in that it requires, as a condition of a government contract, that the employer adhere to a particular clause regarding affirmative action for the disabled and that the order insists on inclusion of that same clause in all subcontracts entered into for the purpose of performance of the government contract. Note, however, that an employer need not adhere to the Executive Order concerning the handicapped unless it has a direct federal contract as opposed to a federally assisted construction project contract. However, participants in federally funded programs are also protected against discrimination even though no affirmative action must be taken.

Executive Order 11701

Whom It Covers

A contractor or subcontractor who has a contract or contracts with the government that equal or exceed $10,000 in any particular year are covered.

Similar to the two above Executive Orders, federal contractors are required to take affirmative action to hire or promote disabled veterans and veterans of the Vietnam era. This additional affirmative action program requires contractors to list vacancies with state employment services and file quarterly reports concerning their employment of veterans.

It should be noted that state employment services are required to give preference to veterans in their referrals. As with the case of the above program, certain contractual clauses must be accepted and adhered to.

Executive Order 11625

Whom It Covers

A contractor or subcontractor who has a contract or contracts with the government that equal or exceed $10,000 in any particular year, are covered.

The minority business enterprise Executive Order operates in the same fashion as the above Orders and essentially requires an employer to agree to certain contract clauses which require affirmative action and non-discrimination.

A federal contractor must meet a number of affirmative action obligations. Meeting those obligations imposes a substantial burden on the employer. Even though employers may not yet be in a situation where they must develop a written affirmative action program, they are required, assuming the employers have contracts of sufficient amount, to adhere to the particular contract clauses which affect them now or which may affect them in the foreseeable future. Employers should also be aware of the requirements because one of their customers might ask them to sign a statement certifying compliance with a particular executive order.

D. The Equal Pay Act

Whom It Covers

Employers whose work involves commerce or production for interstate commerce or who are in an enterprise engaged in commerce.

The Equal Pay Act makes it illegal to pay a female employee lower wages than a male employee for equal work on jobs, the performance of which requires equal skill, effort and responsibility and which are performed under similar working conditions.

Equal work does not necessarily mean *identical* work. Rather, the test is whether the jobs require equal skill, effort and responsibility and whether they are performed under similar working conditions. The test does not depend on the job *classification* or *title* of the individuals involved but on the job *content* consisting of actual job requirements and performance. For example, a male and female may both be classified as stock clerks. However, if the male employee spends the bulk of his work time shifting and moving goods in the stockroom while the female employee spends most of her work time taking inventory and keeping records, the equal pay standard may not apply.

If the pay differential for a salesman and saleswoman is based on economic benefit to the employer from the work performed by each worker, there would be no discrimination. That is, if the employer can demonstrate that the sale of one type of merchandise requires a substantially greater amount of skill than the sale of another type, the job may be considered unequal. In reality, this is rare.

However, if only men are in the higher sales positions the employer will have to demonstrate why females are not in those positions (*e.g.,* women only selling pantyhose, men only selling refrigerators with equal commission rates).

The *equal skill* requirement includes such factors as experience, training, education, and ability, and is measured by actual requirements of the job in question. For example, if an employee must have the same skill to perform either of two jobs, the job would be deemed to require equal skill even though the employee might use a skill less frequently at one job than another. On the other hand, the fact that an employee in a given job possesses certain additional skills is immaterial if the requirements of the job do not require him or her to use that skill. As an illustration, it is entirely possible that you could have a male cashier with a Ph.D. and a female cashier with a high school diploma. The job content in both cases involves operating a cash register. It matters little that one employee has a Ph.D. and the other a high school diploma. You could not compensate the male Ph.D. at a higher rate than the female.

Equal effort entails the amount of physical and mental exertion needed for performance of the job. The effort involved in two jobs need not be identical just be substantially equal. Thus, where a male checker is required to spend a portion of his time carrying or lifting heavy items and a female checker is required to spend an equivalent amount of time in fill-work requiring greater manual dexterity such as rearranging displays of small items, the EEOC deems the jobs to require equal effort.

Equal responsibility is also a component part of determining whether jobs are equal. Responsibility entails the degree of accountability required in the performance of the job with emphasis on the importance of the job obligation. An example of substantial differences in responsibility which would justify differences in pay are individuals designated as relief supervisors who are expected to fill in for regular supervisors in the latter's absence and salespersons who, in addition to their regular selling duties, have the power and obligation to okay customer checks or order supplies, where other salespersons do not have this authority. On the other hand, minor additional responsibilities such as shutting off lights at the end of the business day would not justify a finding of unequal responsibility.

Valid defense for unequal pay in similar jobs can be summarized as follows. You may pay unequal salaries for similar jobs if the salary differentials are based on:

a. a valid seniority system;

b. a valid merit system;

c. a system measuring earnings by quantity or quality of production; and

d. any factor other than sex.

> Remember: You may not reduce the wage of the higher-paid employee to correct an equal pay problem. You must increase the salary of the lower-paid individual.

The Vietnam Era Veterans Readjustment Assistance Act of 1974 and the Rehabilitation Act of 1973

A. "Disabled Veterans" and "Veterans of the Vietnam Era."
Veterans protected under Section 402 of the Vietnam Veterans Act are those who fall within the categories of "disabled veterans" and "veterans of the Vietnam era." A disabled veteran is: a "person entitled to disability compensation under laws administered by the Veterans Administration for disability rated at 30 percent

or more, or a person whose discharge or release from active duty was for a disability incurred or aggravated in the line of duty." A veteran of the Vietnam era is: "a person (1) who (i) served on active duty for a period of more than 180 days, any part of which occurred between August 5, 1964, and May 6, 1975, and was discharged or released therefrom with other than a dishonorable discharge, or (ii) was discharged or released from active duty for a service-connected disability if any part of such active duty was performed between August 5,1964, and May 6,1975, and (2) who was so discharged or released within 48 months preceding the alleged violation of the Act, the affirmative action clause, and/or the regulations pursuant to the Act."

B. "Disabled Individuals"

Only "disabled individuals" are protected by Section 503 of the Rehabilitation Act. A major difficulty encountered by contractors in complying with this law lies in determining which persons fall within this category. It is broadly defined in the Rehabilitation Act to mean "any person who (1) has a physical or mental impairment which substantially limits one or more of such person's major life activities, (2) has a record of such impairment, or (3) is regarded as having such an impairment." Communicable diseases have been held to be disabilities under Section 503 of the Act.

The regulations issued by the Department of Labor further define phrases contained in the statutory definition but do not serve to make it much more concrete. "Substantially limits" refers to the degree that the impairment affects employability. A disabled individual who is likely to experience difficulty in securing, retaining or advancing in employment is considered to be substantially limited. "Life activities" include communication, ambulation, self-care, socialization, education, vocational training, employment, transportation and adapting to housing. Primary attention is given to those life activities that affect employability for purposes of Section 503. "Has a record of such impairment" means that an individual may be completely recovered from a previous physical or mental impairment or may in fact previously have been misclassified as being impaired. Finally, "is regarded as having such impairment" refers to those individuals who are perceived as having a disability, whether impairments exist or not.

The Americans with Disabilities Act

The Americans with Disabilities Act (ADA) was, without question, one of the most sweeping Civil Rights Act to be passed in decades. It is somewhat unique in that it not only forbids discrimination against individuals with disabilities, but it also places an affirmative duty on employers to accommodate those employees to enable them to perform their jobs. This is a very basic introduction to the ADA and the responsibilities it places on employers. In 2008, Congress amended the law in several significant ways. The material that follows incorporates the 2008 Amendment provisions.

The ADA's purpose is to remove the barriers preventing qualified individuals with disabilities from enjoying the same employment opportunities available to persons without disabilities. The ADA does not guarantee equal results, establish quotas, or require an employer to show preference for individuals with disabilities. The ADA does not relieve a disabled person from the obligation to perform the essential functions of a job. All private employers with 15 or more employees are "covered entities."

Disability Defined

Under the amended ADA, a disability is defined as 1) a physical or mental impairment that substantially limits one or more major life activities (an actual disability), 2) a "record" of such an impairment, and 3) being "regarded as" having such an impairment. The EEOC by way of regulations has set forth nine rules that apply when determining whether impairment substantially limits a major life activity:

1. "Substantially limits" will be broadly construed.
2. Compare and individuals limitations against most people in the general population

3. Focus on the employer's compliance obligations and whether discrimination occurred, not whether an individual is substantially lamented by a major life activity.
4. Apply a lower standard during the individualized assessment than existed before the Amendments.
5. Scientific, medical or statistical analysis is not necessary when assessing an individual's performance of a major life function.
6. Do not consider the helpful effects of mitigating measures such as prosthetics, controlling a medical condition with medication (except eyeglasses or contact lenses).
7. An impairment that is episodic or in remission is a disability if it would substantially limit a major life activity when active (*i.e.*, cancer in remission).
8. Only one major life activity needs to be substantially limited to establish the existence of a substantially limiting impairment.
9. Conditions of short duration lasting six months or less may not be substantially limiting (transitory impairment).

As you can see, this makes the claim that much harder for employers to fight.

By "major life activity" the ADA does not raise a very high standard. It contemplates such basic activities as walking, seeing, hearing, speaking, learning, breathing, concentrating, thinking, sleeping, caring for oneself, interacting with others, performing manual tasks, sitting, standing, lifting, and working. Physical disabilities include disfigurement, loss of "a major bodily function," such as reproduction, cardiovascular, skin disorders, endocrine system, urinary system, normal cell growth, bowel, neurological, etc.

Mental Disorders include psychological disorders, organic brain syndrome, emotional or mental illness and learning disabilities.

Note: A person, who can only walk for brief periods of time because of his or her impairment, is substantially limited in a major life activity. A person with a minor or trivial impairment, such as an infected finger, is not impaired in a major life activity.

The statute also now provides that remedial measures are not to be considered when determining "a qualified individual with a disability." Medications, medical supplies, prosthetics, hearing aids and oxygen equipment are examples. So now a diabetic who uses insulin or person with a prosthetic device is covered under the ADA. This provision overruled several Supreme Court cases. Eyeglasses are generally not a mitigating measure, but can be as each case must be evaluated on its own merits.

The "Regarded As" Provision: You May Not "Discriminate on the Basis of a Disability."

The Amendments also provide a new definition of "regarded as having an impairment." <u>An employee is subjected to an action illegal under the Act if the employer takes an adverse action because of an actual or perceived physical or mental impairment, whether or not it limits a major life activity.</u> For instance, let's assume that the employee had a heart attack, which is a covered disability. The employee returns to work without limitations and yet the employer still treats the person as disabled. This is illegal under the "regarded as" provision.

I represented another medical provider who had a nurse practitioner literally pass out in front of a naked patient undergoing a physical. This of course upset the patient. Before allowing the NP to come back to work, the doctor required her to get a release. As it turned out, she had had several brain surgeries, which caused blackouts at unknown times. She filed a charge with the EEOC, claiming that the doctor "regarded her" as disabled because he required medical documentation before she could go back to work. The resulting lawsuit was ultimately resolved, but here was an employer doing what was legal, who still had to defend himself from this claim.

Also note that individuals with a "record of such impairment" are also covered. This is intended to protect individuals who have recovered, or whose disability is in remission, such as cancer patients, AIDS patients, heart attack patients, etc.

Note: An employee whose high blood pressure is controlled by medication, when assigned to a less strenuous work assignment, due to unsubstantiated fears that he will suffer a heart attack, is being regarded by the employer as a disabled individual.

Certain conditions are excluded from the definition of disability. They are:

- "Current illegal drug usage," homosexuality or bi- sexuality, and the following listed mental conditions:
- Transvestism, transsexualism, pedophilia, exhibitionism, voyeurism, gender identity disorders not resulting from physical impairments or other sexual behavior disorders;
- Compulsive gambling, kleptomania, or pyromania, or psychoactive substance use disorders resulting from current illegal use of drugs.

Qualified Individual with a Disability

The ADA does not relieve an individual from performing the essential functions of his or her job. Under the ADA a qualified individual with a disability is an individual with a disability who, with or without reasonable accommodation, can perform the essential functions of the job sought or held.

To determine whether a person is "qualified," an employer must review two things. First, whether the individual possesses the prerequisites for the position, such as education, experience, skill, or licenses; and second, whether or not the disabled person can perform the "essential functions" of a job with or without reasonable accommodation. Essential functions can be determined by ascertaining the fundamental job duties of the position. If a function is required and removing that function would fundamentally change the job, then the function is essential.

What Must the Employer Do?

"Discrimination" includes limiting, segregating, or classifying an applicant or employee in a way that adversely affects his or her opportunities or status because of his or her disability.

Note: It is unlawful under the ADA for an employer to exclude an employee with a severe facial disfigurement from staff meetings because the employer does not like to look at the employee, or for an employer to refuse to hire a person with AIDS.

It is also illegal to use standards, criteria, or tests that exclude all individuals with a disability. However, where such standards or criteria are job related and consistent with business necessity, and the results accurately reflect the skills and qualifications needed for the job, they will be upheld.

It should be noted here that it is an ADA violation to discriminate against an individual because of a relationship to persons with disabilities. This includes not only the family members of the individual, but others associated with the employee as well.

Note: An employer cannot refuse to hire an individual who does volunteer work with AIDS sufferers because of the unfounded fear of contracting the disease.

There is no duty on an employer to accommodate a non disabled person because of his or her relationship to a disabled individual.

Note: An employer cannot refuse to hire an applicant who is married to an individual with cancer because the employer assumes the applicant will miss too much work. However, if after hiring the person violates a neutral attendance policy, the person can be disciplined.

Duty to Make Reasonable Accommodation

It is now illegal under the ADA for employers to fail to provide reasonable accommodation to the known physical or mental limitations of an otherwise qualified individual, or to deny employment to an applicant on the basis of the need to provide reasonable accommodation, unless the employer can demonstrate that the accommodation would impose an undue hardship.

"Reasonable accommodation" means modifications or adjustments (1) to a job application or testing process that enable a qualified applicant with a disability to be considered for the position he or she desires, (2) modifications or adjustments to the work environment or the manner of circumstances in which the job held or desired is customarily performed that enable an individual with a disability to perform the essential functions of the position, or (3) modifications or adjustments that enable an employee with a disability to enjoy equal benefits and privileges of employment as are enjoyed by similarly situated employees without disabilities.

Examples of Reasonable Accommodation:

- Job restructuring
- Part-time or modified work schedules
- Reassignment of employees to "equivalent" vacant positions or to home to do the work
- Acquisition or modification of equipment or devices
- Adjustment or modification of employment ("paper and pencil") tests, training materials or policies
- Provision of qualified readers or interpreters

Accommodating Mental Impairments

The EEOC has stated that mental depression is second only to back injuries as the most common disability in the workplace. The employer must accommodate mental impairments. Any type of modification of job duties, work procedures, or work environment to help the mentally impaired individual may be required. Basic accommodations that are sufficient to meet ADA requirements are:

- Permitting time off for counseling sometimes with pay
- Giving on the job peer counseling
- Allowing telecommuting with the employer's equipment
- Offering job sharing so that workers who cannot handle a full load can still do some work

- Modifying work stations
- Offering sensitivity training

What the Duty to Accommodate Does Not Require

- Alteration of essential functions of the job (in other words an employer is not required to lower quality or quantity standards)
- Bumping an occupied position
- Reassignment of employees to "light duty" positions (unless the individual is able to perform all of the essential functions)
- An employer to supply the employee with personal benefit items (examples: glasses or hearing aids)
- "Supported employment" which are programs to "assist individuals with severe disabilities in both competitive and non-competitive employment"
- Reassignment or accommodation of applicants to other positions
- Holding a job open indefinitely

The Accommodation Process

When a situation that may require accommodation becomes known to an employer, the first step is to look at the particular job involved and determine the purpose and essential functions of the job. Next, consult with the individual to find out his or her specific physical or mental abilities that relate to the essential job functions. This is called the inter-active process and is mandatory.

In consultation with the individual, identify the potential accommodations and assess how effective each would be in enabling the individual to perform the essential job functions. Consider the preference of the individual and settle on the best accommodation for both the individual and employer.

An employer is not required to choose the best accommodation, or the one the individual most prefers. The employer may choose the least expensive or disruptive of the alternatives. If one option is particularly attractive to the individual, but unduly expensive to the employer, the employer can offer to let the individual pay the difference in cost.

Lastly, the employer should carefully document the entire accommodation process.

Undue Hardship on the Employer

The failure to provide reasonable accommodation may be justified where the employer can demonstrate that the accommodation would impose an undue hardship. The hardship is determined on a case-by-case basis, but it must be more than a minimal expense.

"Undue hardship" is defined as any action requiring significant difficulty or expense, taking into account such factors as:

1. The nature and cost of the accommodation required;
2. The overall financial resources of the facility involved in providing the reasonable accommodation;
3. The number of persons employed at the facility;
4. The effect of the reasonable accommodation on expenses and resources;
5. The impact of the accommodation on the operation of the facility;
6. The overall financial resources of the covered entity;
7. The overall size of the covered entity's business with respect to the number of employees;
8. The number, type, and location of its facilities;
9. The type of operation of the covered entity, including the composition, structure, and functions of its work force;
10. The geographic separateness of the facility; and
11. The administrative or fiscal relationship of the facility to the covered entity.

The above list is not exhaustive, nor is a single factor intended to have any particular weight. Rather, all of the factors should be considered in determining whether a proposed accommodation would impose an undue hardship on an employer. Note also, that the cost of the accommodation is figured after considering possible federal assistance or tax credits available.

Direct Threat of Harm

An employer is not required to employ an individual in a position where such employment poses a significant risk to the health or safety of the individual or others that cannot be eliminated or reduced by reasonable accommodation.

To establish that an individual poses a direct threat of harm, an employer must show:

1. The individual with a disability poses a significant risk of substantial harm to himself and/or others;
2. The employer must identify the specific risk;

c. What is the duration of the risk?
   a. What is the duration of the risk?
   b. What is the nature and severity of the potential harm?
   c. What is the likelihood that the potential harm will occur?
   d. What is the imminence of potential harm?

Example: A physician's evaluation of an applicant for a heavy labor job that indicated the individual had a disc condition that might worsen in 8 or 10 years would not be sufficient indication of imminent potential harm.

---

e. The individual with a disability must be a current risk, not a speculative or remote risk.
f. To use this defense, it must be based on objective medical or other factual evidence regarding a particular individual's present ability to safely perform essential functions of the job based upon reasonable current medical judgment.

Note: The ADA prohibits retaliation against an individual for having opposed any act or practice which is unlawful under the ADA or for having made a charge, testified, assisted, or participated in any investigation, proceeding, or hearing under the ADA. Further, it is unlawful to coerce, intimidate, threaten, or interfere with any individual in the exercise or enjoyment of any right granted or protected under the ADA, or any individual having aided or encouraged any other individual in the exercise of their rights under the ADA.

Penalties

The Equal Employment Opportunity Commission has responsibility for investigating charges of discrimination based upon an individual's disability. Thus, the normal Title VII procedures and remedies are available. These remedies include private causes of action in federal court with a jury trial.

ADA Pre-Employment Inquiries – What Can You Ask?

At no time may an employer inquire if the applicant is an individual with a disability, unless such inquiry is job related AND consistent with business necessity. (42 U.S.C. § 12112(d) (2) (A)). Yet you may ask about the ability of an applicant to perform job related essential functions.

1. Before making a job offer, the employer is limited as follows:
   a The Employer may inquire about an applicant's ability to perform specific job functions.
   b The Employer may not inquire about a disability.
   c The Employer may make a conditional job offer based on satisfactory results of a post job offer medical exam or inquiry.
2. After making a conditional offer, but before employee begins work:
   a The Employer may have the employee submit to a medical examination or ask health related questions.

b All candidates who receive a conditional job offer (in the same job type) are required to take the same medical exam or respond to the same health related questions.

  i. All new employees are subjected to the exam regardless of a disability or perceived disability.

  ii. All information you receive must be kept in a separate file, not in the human resource file. All of these medical records must be treated as confidential.

You may not require a physical examination of a current employee unless said exam is job related and consistent with business necessity. You may, however, conduct voluntary medical exams which are part of a health program available to employees at work.

Remember: Whatever you do, the exam or questions must be work related to the essential functions of the job.

The ADA presents a unique challenge to employers. You need to know if the employee can do the job. However, you cannot use a disability against someone who can perform the essential functions of the job, either with or without an accommodation. Nor may you treat someone differently because you think they are disabled.

Family Medical Leave Act

The FMLA became effective August 5, 1993. Final Labor Department regulations were issued in 1995 (29 CFR § 825 et seq.)

Are You Covered?

The FMLA applies to all private sector employers who employ fifty (50) or more employees in twenty or more calendar work weeks in the current or proceeding calendar year and who are engaged in commerce or in any industry or activity affecting commerce.

A. Individual Liability

The Act covers any person who acts directly or indirectly in the interest of an employer to any of the employees of such employer. Many courts have looked to the Fair Labor Standards Act for guidance in ruling on individual supervisor ability. The courts apply Fair Labor Standard Act (FLSA) case law to find that individual supervisors can be liable under the FMLA, if they controlled "in whole or in part" [plaintiff's] ability to take a leave of absence and return to her position. Regulations promulgated under FMLA draw upon the Fair Labor Standards Act, under which individuals "acting in the interest of the employer" can be individually liable. However, some courts have held that individual supervisors are not individually liable. Thus, they are like Title VII supervisors.

B. Employees Covered by the FMLA

Employees eligible for FMLA benefits are those who work for a covered employer for at least a total of twelve months, including a minimum of one thousand two hundred fifty (1250) hours or work for the previous twelve months and who work at a location where at least fifty employees are employed by the employer within seventy-five miles. "Hours of service" should be calculated as they would be under the Fair Labor Standards Act and its regulations, that is, an employee only gets credit for hours actually worked. Time spent on paid or unpaid leave, vacation, holiday, or illness does not count. Employers may deduct previous maternity leave and holidays from "hours of service," which may make the employee ineligible for FMLA leave.

C. Reason for FMLA Leaves

The leave entitlement conferred by the FMLA is a total of twelve work weeks of Unpaid leave during any one year period for one or more of the following reasons:
- For the birth and care of the newborn child of the employee;

- For placement with the employee of a son or daughter for adoption or foster care;
- To care for an immediate family member (spouse, child or parent) with a serious health condition; or
- To take medical leave when the employee is unable to work because of a serious health condition.

The final Department of Labor regulations define a serious health condition as an illness, impairment, or physical or mental condition that is either in-patient care or continuing treatment by a health care provider involving (1) a period of incapacity or treatment in connection with or consequent to inpatient care in a hospital, hospice, or residential medical care facility; (2) a period of incapacity requiring absence from work, school, or other regular daily activities of more than three calendar days, and any subsequent treatment or period of incapacity relating to the same condition, that also involves two or more visits to a health care provider, or at least one visit resulting in a regime of supervised continuing treatment; (3) a period of incapacity due to pregnancy or for prenatal care; (4) a period of incapacity or treatment due to a "chronic" serious health condition that requires periodic visits to a health care provider, that continues over an extended period of time, and may cause episodic rather than continuing periods of incapacity; (5) a period of permanent or long term incapacity due to a condition that may not be responsive to treatment, which requires continual supervision of a health care provider; or (6) a period of absence to receive or recover from multiple treatments by a health care provider or under the orders of a health care provider for restorative surgery after an injury or for a condition likely to result in a period of incapacity of more than three consecutive calendar days in the absence of medical intervention. Minor stomach ulcers are not covered. Other non-serious conditions include colds, flu, and routine dental work.

However, you should note that the Administrator of the Wage and Hour Division of the Department of Labor stated in an opinion letter dated December 12, 1996 (Opinion FMLA-87) that minor complaints such as flu, colds and headaches may qualify an eligible employee for FMLA leave if they incapacitate the employee for more than three calendar days and require treatment by a health care provider. The Final Regulations provide that ordinarily, unless complications arise, the common cold and other minor medical complaints would not be serious health conditions mandating FMLA leave. This Department of Labor opinion letter now suggests that the seriousness of the health condition is no longer relevant, only the length of incapacity and the treatment. The position is at odds with numerous court decisions which appear to place primary consideration on the seriousness of the health condition rather than only the duration and form of treatment.

D.   Military Family Leave Entitlements

Eligible employees with a spouse, son, daughter, or parent on active duty or call to active duty status in the National Guard or Reserves in support of a contingency operation may use their 12-week leave entitlement to address certain qualifying exigencies. Qualifying exigencies may include attending certain military events, arranging for alternative childcare, addressing certain financial and legal arrangements, attending certain counseling sessions, and attending post-deployment reintegration briefings.

FMLA also includes a special leave entitlement that permits eligible employees to take up to 26 weeks of leave to care for a covered service member during a single 12-month period. A covered service member is a current member of the Armed Forces, including a member of the National Guard or Reserves, who has a serious injury or illness incurred in the line of duty on active duty that may render the service member medically unfit to perform his/her duties for which the service member is undergoing medical treatment, recuperation, or therapy; or is in outpatient status; or is on the temporary disability retired list.

E.   Terms of FMLA leave

    1.   Amount of Leave. Eligible employees are entitled to a total of twelve (12) work weeks of FMLA leave during any twelve month period. Leave may be calculated by

any one of four methods. Employers must select a method and apply it consistently and uniformly to all employees. The four methods are: (1) the calendar year; (2) any fixed 12 month "leave year" (such as the employer's fiscal year or a year tied to an employee's anniversary date); (3) a 12 month period measured forward from the date of an employee's first FMLA leave period; or (4) a "rolling "12 month period measured backward from the date an employee uses any FMLA leave. If an employer fails to select one of the four methods, the option that provides the most beneficial outcome for an employee will be used.

2. Intermittent Leave. "Intermittent leave" is defined as any leave taken in separate "blocks of time." A "block of time" can be as short as an hour or as long as several weeks. The regulations state that the employees requiring intermittent FMLA leave must attempt to schedule their leave so as not to disrupt the employer's operations.

An employee may take the 12 weeks of FMLA leave intermittently if the leave is taken to take care of a sick family member or for his/her own illness, if intermittent leave is medically necessary. Employees may not take FMLA leave intermittently for the birth or placement of a new child, unless the employer agrees to such an arrangement. Examples of intermittent leave cited in the final regulations include: leave taken on an occasional basis for medical appointments; leave taken several days at a time spread over a long period of time, such as for chemotherapy; and leave that reduces an employee's usual number of working hours per work week or per work day.

3. Compensation During Leave. The FMLA leave requirement generally refers to unpaid leave, but, subject to certain conditions, employees or employers may choose to substitute accrued paid sick or vacation leave to cover some or all of the FMLA leave.

If an employee is taking FMLA leave for the birth or placement of a new child, the employee may elect, or the employer may require, substitution of any applicable accrued paid vacation leave, personal leave or family leave for the unpaid leave benefit under the Act. If an employee is taking FMLA leave either to care for a spouse, child, or parent with a serious health condition or to recover from his or her own serious health condition, the employee may elect, or the employer may require, substitution of any applicable accrued paid vacation leave, personal leave, family leave, or sick/medical leave for the unpaid leave benefit under the Act. When paid leave is substituted for unpaid leave, the leave period may be counted against the employee's 12 week FMLA leave allotment as long as the leave otherwise qualifies as FMLA leave.

Among a series of minor corrections and clarifications to the FMLA regulations issued by the Labor Department's Wage and Hour Division in March of 1995, was a ruling allowing FMLA leave entitlement to run concurrently with a workers' compensation absence "when the injury is one that meets the criteria for a serious health condition."

4. Benefits During Leave. The employer is required to maintain the employee's coverage under any group health plan during all FMLA leaves on the same conditions as if the employee had been continuously employed during the leave period. All components of a group health benefit plan must be maintained during an FMLA leave including medical, surgical, hospital, dental and eye care, mental health counseling, and substance abuse treatment. Any group health plan changes applicable to all employees must apply to employees on FMLA leave and notice of any opportunity to change plans or benefits must also be afforded any employee on FMLA leave. However, the employee must also continue their contributions if any to the plan.

What Rights Does the Employee Have?

An employee who takes a qualified FMLA leave is entitled, upon return from such leave, to be restored to the same or an "equivalent" position with the same seniority rights and benefits the employee had when the leave commenced. The regulations define an "equivalent position" as one that has virtually identical pay, benefits, and working conditions (including privileges, perquisites and status) as the position held by the employee prior to taking FMLA leave. Specifically, the position must involve the same or substantially similar duties and responsibilities, which must entail substantially equivalent skill, effort, responsibility, and authority. An employee's right to reinstatement is co-extensive with the rights the employee would have had if the employee had been working during the leave period. If the employee's position was eliminated or substantially changed during the leave period, the employee has no right to reinstatement to his or her position or working conditions. The general rule is that the FMLA is not a strict liability statute and confers no additional rights or benefits on employees than they would have enjoyed had they not requested leave.

An employer cannot deny a "key employee" (e.g., one who is among the highest paid 10% of all the employees employed within a 75 mile radius of the facility at which the employee works) the right to take FMLA leave. However, the Act allows an employer to deny such an employee reinstatement if: (a) job restoration will "result in substantial and grievous economic injury" to the employer; and (b) the employer provides written notice to the key employee of its intent to deny reinstatement. What the employer must show to deny restoration is that reinstating the employee will cause substantial and grievous economic injury. This standard makes the "key employee" exemption so difficult to establish that it is of little or no practical value.

If an employee fails to return from a qualified FMLA leave upon exhaustion of his or her allotted 12 weeks, the employer may obtain reimbursement from the employee for the group health coverage premiums paid by the employer during the leave if:

1. The employee's reason for not returning is not related to the continuance, recurrence, or onset of a serious health condition which would have entitled the employee to FMLA leave; or

2. The employee's reason for not returning is not related to "other circumstances beyond the employee's control."

Who Must Give Notice?

1. <u>Employee's Notice Obligations</u>.

Employees are required to give their employer thirty (30) days notice of their intent to take FMLA leave, or as much as is "practicable." The courts have been confronted with a number of cases that turn on the adequacy of the notice provided. Some courts have also held that employees who take time off for unforeseeable situations covered by the FMLA need not expressly mention the Act when they notify their employers of the need for leave. The final regulations, which took effect in April 1995, resolved any ambiguity by making clear that mention of the FMLA by name is not required for unforeseen leave.

The general notice rule is that adequate notice is that which provides sufficient detail to make it evident that the requested leave was protected as FMLA qualifying leave. An employer should not have to speculate as to the nature of an employee's condition. Sometimes all an employer has is a doctor's note. For instance, the doctor's excuse may only state "please excuse (employee) of work until (dates)." This is sufficient to trigger the employer's duty to make further inquiry to determine if the leave is qualified under the FMLA. If leave is taken for an FMLA covered reason of which the employer is not aware, the employee must notify the employer of the reason for the leave within two business days of returning to work, in order to invoke the Act's protection.

Prior to granting an employee FMLA leave, the employer may require that the employee produce written certification from a health care provider of the employee's serious health condition. Form WH-308 has been provided by the Labor Department for employer's use. If the employer has reason to doubt the validity of the certification provided, the employer may require, at the employer's expense, that the eligible employee obtain the opinion of a second health care provider designated or approved by the employer. If there is a conflict in the two opinions, a third opinion may be obtained at the employer's expense. However, the third health care provider must be agreed upon by the parties, and his/her opinion is final.

2. Employer's Notice Obligations
   a Posted Notice. A covered employer must post notices that explain the FMLA's provisions and procedures for filing complaints of violations of the Act in conspicuous areas of the employer's premises. The Department of Labor has prepared a notice form for use by employers.
   b Update Policies. A covered employer must also supplement any handbooks, manuals and written policies with information about FMLA entitlements and obligations.
   c Specific Notice. Once an employee notifies his or her employer of a request for FMLA qualifying leave, the employer must provide written information to the employee concerning the employer's particular expectations and requirements and the consequences of failing to comply with such requirements. This information should include the following:
      i.   Notice that the leave will count against the employee's 12-week entitlement;
      ii. Whether the employer requires certification of a serious health condition and the consequences of failing to provide such certification;
      iii. The employee's right to substitute paid leave, whether the employer will require such substitution and any conditions related to substitution of paid leave;
      iv. Any requirement for the employee to make premium payments for health benefits, the arrangements for making such payments, and the

consequences of failing to make the payments in a timely manner;

v. Whether the employer will require the employee to provide a fitness for duty certificate to be restored to employment;

vi. Whether the employee is a "key employee" and the potential consequence that he or she will not be restored to employment, including an explanation of the conditions for denial;

vii. The employee's right to restoration to the same or equivalent position upon return from leave; and

viii. The employee's potential liability for payment of health insurance premiums paid by the employer during any unpaid FMLA leave period if the employee fails to return to work.

It is essential for employers to provide this individualized notice to employees on a timely basis. FMLA regulations imply that, absent limited exceptions, leave taken before the individualized notice is provided cannot be counted against an employee's annual entitlement to 12 work weeks of FMLA leave. Thus, for example, an employee who takes 12 weeks of FMLA qualifying leave and returns to work without having received an individualized notice must be treated as if he or she has taken no FMLA leave at all.

Failure to Comply with Notice Requirements

Failure to post the required notice can result in assessment of a civil money penalty not to exceed $100 for each separate offense, to be enforced by the Department of Labor, and the non-posting employer may be stopped from taking adverse action against an employee who fails to furnish advance notice of the need for FMLA leave. Neither provision contemplates damages to the adversely affected employee.

Enforcing the FMLA

The Act gives employees the right either to file an administrative complaint with the Department of Labor or to file a civil action for monetary damages and equitable remedies (*e.g.* employment, reinstatement of employment, or promotion) against employers who violate the law. There is no requirement of exhaustion of administrative remedies. Moreover, even if the plaintiff files a DOL charge, he or she may still file a civil action at any time within the statute of limitations as long as the Secretary of Labor has not yet initiated litigation in the matter. In court cases, liquidated damages are also available where it is proven that the employer has interfered with, restrained, or denied the exercise of the rights under the Act, or has discriminated or retaliated against an employee for exercising his/her rights. Emotional distress damages are not available. Lawsuits must be filed within two (2) years of the employer's last violation of the Act, or three (3) years if the violation was willful.

Where an employee prevails in a civil lawsuit, he/she may also recover costs and reasonable attorneys' fees.

The FMLA also provides for administrative enforcement by the filing of a complaint with the Secretary of Labor.

Sexual Harassment

Many courts refused to recognize sexual harassment as being illegal sex discrimination when these suits were first started. The judges were afraid that every disgruntled female employee would charge the company with harassment. Because of the devastating nature of a false charge on a male supervisor, both personally and professionally, the courts were reluctant to recognize a valid cause of action. Further, some felt that because a company had policies against this conduct, sexual harassment was merely the unsanctioned activity of a particular supervisor. They would, thus, not hold the company liable for the damages caused. However, now the actions of a supervisor are generally held to be those of the company and there will be liability for his or her actions.

It may be best to begin with the EEOC guidelines. These provide that unwelcome sexual advances, requests for sexual favors, and other physical or verbal conduct of a sexual nature will be considered harassment if:

1. Submission to such conduct is made either explicitly or implicitly a term or condition of an individual's employment,
2. Submission to or rejection of such conduct by an individual is used as the basis for employment decisions affecting such individual, or
3. Such conduct has the purpose or effect of unreasonably interfering with an individual's work performance or creating an intimidating, hostile, or offensive working environment.

The EEOC interprets these guidelines imposing three different standards of liability on the employer, depending upon the parties involved. These guidelines actually define two types of sexual harassment: hostile atmosphere/environment and "quid pro quo" or trading sex for job benefits.

A. Supervisors.

Employers will be held liable for acts of supervisors or agents "regardless of whether the specific acts complained of were authorized or even forbidden by the employer and regardless of whether the employer knows or should have known of their occurrence if a tangible employment action occurs (e.g., economic harm)." This standard would hold an employer liable for the actions of a supervisor even if the employer had no knowledge of those actions because the supervisor is held to "be" the employer. An employee is a "supervisor" for this purpose only if he or she is empowered by the employer to take tangible employment actions against an employee (i.e. hiring, firing, demotion, promotion).

The Supreme Court of the United States decided that the company is only liable for the acts of the supervisor if the supervisor is acting in the scope of his or her employment. However, that has been expanded. The company will always be held liable as long as some job detriment can be seen in the actions of the supervisor. It is important to note that the Court clearly said that hostile work atmosphere harassment is actionable under Title VII. The Court held, "For sexual harassment to be actionable, it must be sufficiently severe or pervasive to alter the conditions of the victim's employment and create an abusive environment." That means that one comment probably wouldn't be sexual harassment. However, one certainly would argue that rape or touching of private areas is sexual harassment.

Further, the EEOC takes the position that if an employee is denied employment opportunities or benefits because he or she refused sexual advances, and those benefits were granted to an employee who did acquiesce, the first employee may bring a charge of sexual discrimination against the company. It is important to note that even though the plaintiff has a cause of action under Title VII of the Civil Rights Act, he or she may also sue both the company and the supervisor (or fellow employee) personally for emotional distress and psychological damages under various State law theories. Generally, these cases are brought under state, not federal laws. Therefore, it is extremely important that all incidents or allegations of sexual harassment be investigated promptly and thoroughly.

The U.S. Supreme Court also clarified the company's liability when an employee is harassed by a supervisor, but the employee didn't tell anyone. The Court held that an employer is vicariously liable for actionable discrimination caused by the supervisor, even if the employer didn't know. However, the employer has an affirmative defense. It can show that its actions as a company were reasonable and that of the victim were not. This translates to a defense to a claim by showing that the company had a strong policy against harassment in place, coupled with a complaint and investigation procedure. If the employee/victim doesn't avail herself/himself of the procedure, the employer can use that as a defense. Therefore, an employer *must* do two very important things:

1. Have a strong policy against discrimination and harassment and publish it to all employees; and
2. Have a complaint procedure whereby the employee can make complaints. That procedure must identify a person to whom the employee may complain if the supervisor is the alleged offender.

After an investigation, the employer must then take <u>effective remedial action</u>. This new affirmative defense is available only in the case where there is only a hostile environment and no tangible employment action (demotion, termination, lack of promotion, etc.) is taken against the employee. The defense is comprised of two elements:

1. The employer exercised reasonable care to prevent and correct promptly any sexually harassing behavior (policy, complaint procedure, effective remedial action); and
2. That the employee unreasonably failed to take advantage of any preventative or corrective opportunities provided by the employer or to otherwise avoid harm.

In other words, did the employee use the complaint procedure and if not, was it reasonable for the victim to fail to complain under the circumstances?

Note: This defense is not available if the employee suffers some tangible detriment to his/her employment.

The Court in another case held that an employee who refuses the unwelcome and threatening sexual advances of a supervisor, yet suffers no adverse tangible job consequences, can recover against the employer without showing the employer is negligent or otherwise at fault for the supervisor's actions. That means a simple hostile environment case will lead to damages if the supervisor is the harasser, even if no one in the company was told by the victim.

This is important because the employee must prove harassment is "severe or pervasive" in a hostile environment claim (no detrimental employment actions). However, when the employee proves a detrimental employment action as a result of refusing to submit to a supervisor's sexual demands, the adverse employment decision alone is actionable under Title VII. This is because there is a change in the terms and conditions of employment. In this case the Court defined "tangible employment action" as one which constitutes a significant change in employment status, such as hiring, firing, demotion, failing to promote, reassignment with significantly different responsibilities, or a decision causing a significant change in benefits.

The Court decided that when it comes to the company's liability for the acts of its supervisors, the distinctions of *quid pro quo* sexual harassment and hostile work environment harassment will not matter. When the supervisor created a hostile work environment by making threats to alter the workplace, but never carried them out, the employee quit, alleging a constructive discharge. The Court then reiterated its holding that an employer will be liable for a hostile work environment created by its supervisors even if the employer didn't know–subject to the affirmative defenses stated above.

The best defense is that you have taken appropriate corrective action. You've granted the lost benefits, or removed the supervisor, transferred the employee (not the best course of action, but may be the only one) or the alleged harasser (a much better alternative to moving the victim) or done a myriad of other things to change the situation. You must stop the harassment and bring the work environment back into a pleasant non-hostile condition.

In order for an employee to prove sexual harassment, he or she must produce credible evidence (either witnesses or documentary evidence) of the illegal acts. The Court will look at the "totality of the circumstances." That means it will scrutinize the actions of both parties. The actions of consenting adults are not sexual harassment. It may become sexual harassment if the employee breaks off the relationship and the supervisor then uses the employment situation to obtain more sexual favors (or punishes the employee on the job for breaking off the affair).

An employee does not have to suffer economic harm, or loss of employee benefits or promotions, etc. It is enough if he or she can show that a hostile sexual environment exists. Therefore, a cause of action exists for sex discrimination when the employee's "psychological and emotional work environment" was "poisoned" by sexual harassment, insults, and demeaning proposition.

However, the Supreme Court gave employers further guidance on the issue. The Court laid out two tests:

1. The Objective Test: would a reasonable person find the conduct complained of to create a "hostile or abusive" work environment.
2. The Subjective Test: if the victim does not subjectively perceive the environment to be abusive, the conduct has not actually altered the conditions of the victim's employment.

However some courts have held that the standard should be a "reasonable woman," not a reasonable "person." In any event, if an employee makes a complaint of sexual harassment, you can bet she (or he) has passed the "subjective" test.

Remember: In a hostile environment case, a victim must prove the conduct was so severe and pervasive as to change the working conditions or terms of employment.

Since passage of the 1991 Civil Rights Act (CRA), victims of discrimination under Title VII can get a jury trial. Damages for emotional distress, loss of enjoyment of life, and inconvenience can be awarded to victims of sexual harassment. Further, a jury can now award punitive damages. This significantly ups the ante on these cases and employers must do everything in their power to thoroughly investigate the complaint and take effective remedial action.

The damages of this type are capped by the 1991 CRA as follows:

3. 15–100 employees, $50,000
4. 101–200 employees, $100,000
5. 201–500 employees, $200,000
6. Over 500 employees, $300,000

These amounts are in addition to back pay, reinstatement, or in lieu thereof, front pay and attorneys' fees.

B. <u>Fellow Employees</u>.

The employer's liability also extends to actions of other employees, but employer knowledge is a requirement in these situations. Employers are considered responsible for acts of sexual harassment between fellow employees when they "know or should have known of the conduct," unless it can be shown that the employer took "immediate and appropriate corrective action." Therefore, the employee must inform the employer of the conduct of the fellow employee. However, if a supervisor witnesses the illegal actions by or between employees, the company will be held to have "known." It must then take corrective action, up to and including discharge of the offender.

What about the person who is actually the "aggressor" or "initiator" of the sexual conduct and then charges the company with discrimination? The courts have uniformly held that when the employee "welcomes" the advances or initiates them, no liability exists. After all, the key is that the conduct must be unwelcome. The employee's conduct is admissible to prove that the actions complained of were welcome. The Supreme Court has held that a woman's mode of dress and actions can show that she was not or would not be offended. In a case where the plaintiff initiated sex-related jokes, and sexual horseplay, the court held this as evidence that the conduct complained of was welcome. Moreover, the use of foul language, rude comments, off-color jokes and the like will not in and of themselves be considered sexual harassment. The conduct must be sexually oriented, utilized in the presence of women and not similarly done in the presence of men and it must be unwelcome.

I represented a woman who was subjected to sexual comments by her co-workers: all women. They would talk about their sex lives, tell dirty jokes and even though my client was not addressed specifically, she was offended just listening. She complained to the manager, who replied that that was "just the girls talking." The case was settled in my client's favor because it was obvious that she was subjected to a "hostile offensive environment" and the employer didn't take "effective remedial action" to stop the offensive language <u>even though nothing was ever addressed to her.</u>

C. General Public.

The employer also has potential liability for the actions of non-employees (customers/clients, delivery persons, copy repair people other vendors, etc.) in cases of harassment in the workplace. In cases of this type, the EEOC will consider the extent of the employer's control and any other legal responsibility of the employer regarding non-employees. The guidelines state that such situations will be considered on a case-by-case basis.

The law also imposes liability on the employer if it places the employee in a position where he or she will be sexually harassed and the employer could have controlled the situation but did not. The courts have allowed causes of action for sexual harassment when dress codes in an office building and in an airport lounge required the wearing of revealing clothes that caused employees to be the objects of sexual harassment by customers.

D. Same Sex Harassment.

The U.S. Supreme Court decided that same sex harassment is illegal under Title VII of the Civil Rights Act. A male employee was subjected to incredible acts of harassment by male co-workers (who were not gay). Thus, activities such as physically assaulting the employee in a sexual manner, threatening the employee with rape and various sexually related comments, are illegal even if perpetrated by a male or males on another male.

The cases are clear that homosexual advances by a male or female supervisor against same gender employees is definitely illegal under Title VII.

E. __Constructive Discharge.__

If an employee should resign because the company would do nothing about the offensive conduct, the courts will treat said voluntary resignation as an involuntary termination. This will subject the company to the same liability as if it had fired the person or abolished his or her job.

Courts will generally impose either or both of two standards on the plaintiff. The plaintiff will need to show that the conduct complained of was so outrageous and intolerable that he or she had to quit. The standard used by most courts is whether a reasonable person would have quit under similar circumstances. In some jurisdictions the plaintiff must show that a discriminatory workplace was the reason he or she quit.

F. __Company Policies.__

It is no defense to have a strong policy against sexual harassment and claim that the guilty supervisor, by violating it, was outside the scope of his or her employment and not do anything about the harassment. The Courts have routinely held that just having a policy against sexual harassment is not the determinative factor. In one case, even though the employer had an extensive EEO training program for its managers and supervisors, the court still held the company liable, because it did not take strong enough corrective action.

Therefore, merely having a policy without enforcement is tantamount to none at all. Enforcement of the policy and quick appropriate action when a violation is found are the keys. Management must constantly monitor the situation and the shifting personalities in the workplace. Giving lip service to a policy will only get your company in trouble.

G. Complaint Procedure.

It is important, too, to provide a complaint mechanism by which people can bring sexual harassment complaints and have them fairly investigated without the fear of reprisal. There must be a guarantee of an atmosphere free of reprisal for making the complaint. The importance of this cannot be stressed enough. No employee will use the complaint mechanism if he or she has no confidence in it or will be retaliated against because he or she has complained.

Remember: Even though the company may not be guilty of the alleged harassment, if the complainant or witnesses are retaliated against, the employer will be guilty under Title VII for retaliation.

H. Elements of a Good Harassment Policy.

1. Identify all prohibited conduct and specifically identify **sexual harassment** or granting benefits to romantic or sexual partners or relationships.
2. Have an identifiable **complaint procedure.**
3. Have a **separate policy** for managers and supervisors.
4. **Train managers** on what is acceptable in the workplace, to identify unacceptable conduct, and how to handle complaints.
5. **Investigate promptly,** thoroughly and engage in no retaliation.
6. Take immediate **"effective remedial action"** up to and including termination (although termination is not required-only that the offending conduct stop).

Sample sex harassment policies are included in the appendix.

I. Conclusion.

Sexual harassment allegations are made easily and are extremely damaging to an individual supervisor and the company as a whole. It is important that management create a work atmosphere that discourages sexual harassment in any form. It is equally important to correct problems as they come up and to investigate each incident thoroughly. Not only will an in-depth investigation prepare the company for defending the charge or lawsuit, it will also set a precedent for others by proving that management cares to investigate and to correct the situation.

On the other hand, managers and supervisors are not guilty until proven innocent. If your employees are cleared of wrongdoing, good management principles dictate that the employer stick by them. Don't sell them short. They have families and can be harmed irreparably by these false accusations. A thorough investigation also gives your managers and supervisors confidence that the company will be fair in making its evaluation. Whatever the outcome, once management has all the necessary facts and information, take corrective action before the employee files the charge. If the charge is already filed, take corrective action immediately.

Finally, if the person has quit, if you offer that person reinstatement even without back pay, you have limited your liability to damages up to the date of the offer.

Remember: Fast corrective action will limit or eliminate your liability.

Pregnancy

One aspect of sex discrimination that has been disputed for many years is whether or not employment decisions based on an employee's pregnancy are sex discrimination. Prior to 1978 the U.S. Supreme Court held that employment classifications based on pregnancy were not sex discrimination.

However, in 1978 Title VII of the Civil Rights Act of 1964 was amended by the Pregnancy Discrimination Act which states in part:

(k) "The terms 'because of sex' or on the 'basis of sex' include but are not limited to, because or on the basis of pregnancy, childbirth or related medical conditions; and women affected by pregnancy shall be treated the same for all employment purposes:" (42 USC §2000e, as amended).

In short, employers may not discriminate or make employment decisions solely because an employee is pregnant. One must go much farther before adverse action against the employee may be taken.

Many employers have tried to prove that pregnant women will have an adverse impact on customer relations. They argue that this is a legitimate business reason for terminating or laying off pregnant workers. The courts have uniformly rejected that as not a bona fide reason. I represented a pregnant bartender who was fired from her job simply because she was pregnant. The bar owner said that he "worried for her safety" on the slippery floor behind the bar. He also said that when she became pregnant she didn't fit into the "look" he wanted for the bar. They had the reputation for having the "prettiest girls in town," and when she became pregnant, she lost that "look." Needless to say we won that case, as the court didn't buy any of that as a bona fide occupational qualification.

However, what if the pregnant employee cannot physically do the work legitimately assigned to her? Management must make an attempt at a reasonable accommodation just as it would for any other physically handicapped person. If the employee's physician allows her to continue her duties, the employer may not legitimately restrict her activities. If no reasonable accommodation can be made, the employee may be removed from her position. Before management relieves someone of her duties because of its belief that she is physically unable to do the work, it would be wise to have her examined by your company physician or one of your choosing. In this way, if the physician states that she should not or cannot perform her duties, the company will have a legitimate business reason to restrict her duties or put her on a leave of absence.

> *Remember:* This leave may not be more restrictive than leave granted for other injuries or disabilities. There is no requirement that companies have a paid leave policy, but if they do, it must apply to all disabilities equally including pregnancy.

What if the company is concerned for the health of the mother or the fetus? A federal appeals court addressed the issue of whether a hospital can fire an X-ray technician when she becomes pregnant to protect the pregnant employee's fetus from potentially harmful radiation and to protect the hospital's finances from potential litigation. The Court rejected the hospital's arguments that the policy to terminate was a legitimate business necessity. The Court began its analysis with the presumption that "...if the employer's policy by its terms applies only to women or pregnant women, the policy is facially discriminatory." The Court found no reason advanced by the hospital to believe that the harm to the health of the fetus or the potential for lawsuits against it were legitimate reasons for terminating pregnant employees.

The Court required that there be "a direct relationship between the policy and the actual ability of a pregnant or fertile female to perform her job." The Court refused to hold that exposure to civil tort suits was a legitimate business necessity.

The Supreme Court weighed in on **fetal protection policies** in a case where a company that made batteries banned all women of child-bearing age from working in certain jobs. They were worried that women in these jobs had excessive lead levels in their blood. The Court held that this was discrimination under the Pregnancy Discrimination Act (PDA). The Court said that the policy was not neutral because it didn't apply to men. The holding confirmed that the actual pregnancy must interfere with the job, not the ability to bear children or any potential danger to the mother or a fetus.

Therefore, companies must have a neutral policy dealing with all types of disability. Pregnancy must be treated as other disabilities in that once it has been shown objectively that the pregnant employee cannot physically meet the demand of the position, she may be terminated or placed on a leave of absence under the standard policies and procedures in effect at that time.

Must Employers Rehire?

Always remember that pregnancy is covered under the Family Medical Leave Act and so a woman will get 12 weeks of leave and her job is protected. The law does not require preferential treatment–only equal treatment in granting the leave in the first place. You will be held to the same standard as any other medical leave you allow.

Remember: If you have a policy of keeping positions open or offering comparable jobs to employees with illnesses or disabilities other than pregnancy, then you must do the same for returning female employees after childbirth.

Religious Discrimination

As you know, one of the protected classes under Title VII is "religion." The Supreme Court has held that employers must "reasonably accommodate" employees' religious beliefs. However, the test is not so stringent as in ADA cases. For instance the Court did not make an airline revamp its seniority policy in order to accommodate someone's Sabbath. An employer is not expected to engage in undue hardship in order to accommodate someone's religious beliefs. The employer need not accommodate the beliefs, if the hardship is more than "*de minimus*" (slight). The employer need not discriminate against other employees to accommodate the religious beliefs of one employee.

Polygraph Tests

Before an employer contemplates the use of a lie detector test or other truth and deception devices, it should carefully review the law in its state. For instance, in Nebraska the lie detector test results cannot be the sole determinative factor in any employment decision. Also, before it can be administered, the employee or applicant must agree in writing to take it. A full scale review of every state law is beyond the scope of this book. Always check with your attorney before implementing a polygraph policy or program.

The Genetic Information Non-Discrimination Act of 2008 (GINA)

The Genetic Information Non-Discrimination Act by a nearly unanimous Congress to prohibit employment discrimination based on "genetic information." It became effective in November 2009. The EEOC issued regulations in November 2010. There are three sections: Title I prohibits genetic discrimination by insurers, Title II prohibits genetic discrimination in employment, and Title III which has several miscellaneous provisions. Employers with 15 or more employees are covered.

The goal of Title II is to prohibit discrimination in employment based on one's genetic information. This includes hiring, firing pay, job assignments, promotions, layoffs and any other "conditions" of employment. Harassment and retaliation is prohibited against anyone filing a charge. Title II also prohibits employers from forcing employees to undergo genetic testing. And finally, it prohibits employers from disseminating any genetic information already in its possession.

Exceptions to disclosing fall into six categories:

1. The employer obtained the information inadvertently.
2. The information was obtained on a voluntary basis, as part of a health or genetic service.
3. The information was obtained in the form of a medical history when complying with a law (*i.e.*, FMLA or state and local laws on leaves).
4. The information is already public.
5. The information is required to be provided by law.
6. The information is obtained by employees who conduct DNA testing for law enforcement purposes or for the purpose of identifying human remains.

If you have access to this information, you must keep it in a separate file.

The definitions of employer and employee are according to Title VII of the Civil Rights Act. However, there is no individual liability; only the company can be held liable. Yet the remedies provided under Title VII are given to employees whose rights are violated.

I recommend that a GINA policy be in every employer handbook.

Social Media and the National Labor Relations Board

Employees are embracing social media such as Facebook, Twitter, LinkedIn, etc. It is extremely common for employees to complain about and attack their employers on these sites. You must be extremely cautious before terminating an employee who has posted negative things about you, your managers or the company. Almost every employer is covered under the National Labor Relations Act (NLRA or "the Act"). Only the smallest employer which doesn't get any goods or services in interstate commerce may be exempt. Even then check with your lawyer to see if the Act applies to you. The Board takes a very liberal stance, trying to include as many employers as possible under its umbrella. Some states are now enacting laws prohibiting employers from asking for private passwords to Facebook and other social media sites.

The NLRA applies to a variety of situations regarding your employees even if you are non-union. The Act was enacted to protect employees who engage in "protected concerted activity" over wages, hours and working conditions. Concerted activity is when 1) one employee speaks on behalf of him/herself and one or more employees; 2) two or more employees discuss issues such as safety concerns, benefits or any working condition; or 3) two or more employees addressing their employer about pay. The NLRA covers an incredibly diverse range of conduct and topics. For instance the following are examples of areas covered: wages, hours, working conditions (even something as insignificant as poor lighting over a desk), performance, discipline, supervisory conduct, etc.

It is illegal for an employer to "chill" these rights or to take action in retaliation for exercising them. The National Labor Relations Board (NLRB) has taken a hard line against employers who terminate employees who post things about their working conditions on social media. Also, the Board has taken a dim view of almost every employer's social media policy on which they have ruled. Any comments that can reasonably be interpreted as applying to the employee and the co-workers are concerted activity. However, "personal gripes" that only deal with the single employee are not protected.

Policies that prohibit employees from being "disrespectful" and prohibiting comments that "damage the company, defame any individual or damage a person's reputation" have been held to violate the Act according to the Board. Therefore, it is imperative that if you feel an employee is disparaging your company on a social media site, that you seek legal advice **before** terminating or disciplining the employee. The Appendix has a social media policy that was approved by the Board as of the time of publication of this book. It is imperative that you have a policy in writing, so that all employees understand that they have rights, but that you do too.

Recordkeeping Requirements

This area has many pitfalls. For instance the Department of Labor can go back three years for a willful violation under the Fair Labor Standards Act. Thus, you must have all employee pay records for a minimum of three years.

Immigrations forms, such as I-9's must be retained as long as the employee is employed and then at least a year after that. These must be kept in a separate locked cabinet away from the general employee files.

It is beyond the scope of this book to detail every record retention requirement. However, I recommend that all employment records be kept a minimum of seven years from the date of the employee's termination.

Post-Employment Claims – They Can Hurt You

Post-employment claims such as unemployment compensation, disability, labor arbitration, workers' compensation, etc., must be treated very seriously by management. These "insignificant" claims, normally routine, can become pivotal in future litigation long after the unemployment claim is forgotten. This is because they usually occur well in advance of discrimination charges or suits for unjust dismissal. Claims are handled routinely by a supervisor or HR department staff person without regard to the record made. This is a big mistake! The courts are holding that testimony under oath in administrative proceedings can be used to impeach later testimony or used as an admission against the employer.

Even more significant is that some courts have held that the findings of fact made by an administrative agency can be conclusive on the parties in later proceedings (collateral estoppel). That is, the parties cannot again litigate the same issue and facts because they have already been decided by a competent authority after a hearing.

Finally, results of EEOC, unemployment compensation tribunals, etc., in some state and federal courts may be offered into evidence "for whatever they're worth," which is determined by the jury or judge. Many times the jury can be swayed into believing that the decision of the administrative agency is to be given great weight. Therefore, the employer must make a choice very early, sometimes before it even has an indication of discrimination problems or before it has hired a lawyer. You must choose to fight the claim or forget it and wait for the big battle. If the employer chooses to fight a clear-cut unemployment compensation misconduct case for example, it should do so with full documentation and an eye to future litigation.

Let's assume a female has been terminated for stealing and she applies for unemployment benefits. Do you contest that case? Of course. What if you put a male employee on probation for stealing six months ago? If you admit that at the unemployment hearing, it can be later used against you in a sex discrimination (disparate treatment) case.

To protect your company in all situations, follow these rules:

1. Keep the issues as narrow as possible. Do not let the claimant or the hearing officer wander into irrelevant territory.
2. Do not make admissions on the record that will be harmful in a later case.
3. Do not participate in administrative proceedings unless you want to make a record for a potentially larger case.
4. During the administrative proceeding, establish a record that you have not had the opportunity for full procedural due process (*i.e.*, full discovery, inability to call witnesses, rules of evidence not applied, inability to cross-examine witnesses, etc.).
5. Many times the standards and burdens of proof in agencies vary from what courts require (most often the formal rules of evidence do not apply). Therefore, make a record as to what the burden of proof is for that agency. In other words, the standard to prove constructive discharge in unemployment hearings may be very minimal. The finding against you on the issue should arguably not be held conclusive in a wrongful discharge case. Many courts have held that evidence and admissions can be used against you, but the conclusion may not because the burden of proof is different in discrimination cases (as opposed to unemployment cases).

In summary, the employer must analyze the potential for future litigation, even prior to termination of the employee. Only then can management adequately protect itself in the early post-termination proceedings.

If You Are Found Guilty of Violating These Equal Employment Opportunity/Discrimination Laws

If you are found guilty of violating the EEOC/Discrimination laws you may be required to do any or all of the following:

1. Reinstate a discharged employee and pay him/her back pay from the date of termination.
2. Pay an employee found to have been denied a promotion the difference in pay between his/her actual earnings and what he/she would have earned had the promotion not been denied.
3. Place the discharged employee on a preferential waiting list and place that person at the earliest possible time.
4. Train the person you are ordered to hire or promote if that has been your practice with prior employees.
5. Restructure, build or otherwise alter your building to accommodate certain disabilities.
6. Be found guilty of violation of criminal statutes.
7. Relinquish any further furnishings of your product to schools, hospitals, public buildings and the like.
8. Establish how many minorities, females, etc., you must hire in certain periods.
9. Allow the government to review your books and records as to whom you hire, promote, train, etc., on a periodic basis.
10. Change your present lines of promotion progression.
11. Change your pay differentials.
12. Prepare and follow an entire Affirmative Action Program and update it yearly.
13. Hire and promote in all levels and departments on a percentage basis to conform to Standard Metropolitan Statistical Area (percentage of minorities in your area).
14. Pay back pay, front pay, punitive damages.
15. Pay damages for emotional distress, loss of enjoyment of life.
16. Pay the possibly huge legal fees for the people (minorities, females, others) who have sued you for discrimination.

The Prima Facie Case and Its Defense

Before beginning the internal investigation of a charge of discrimination, the employer must know what the charging party needs to prove and what the defense burdens will be.

The U.S. Supreme Court has laid out the allocation of the burdens of proof and defense in Title VII cases. The burdens will be somewhat different in disparate impact and disparate treatment cases.

Disparate Impact – *Prima Facie* Case

We touched upon this earlier, but I want to make this very clear. Under the disparate impact analysis, the Charging Party must show, by a preponderance of the evidence, that the challenged practice has a significant discriminatory impact. It is not necessary to show discriminatory intent.

The burden then shifts to the employer to defend its action and justify its policy. The employer-defendant must demonstrate that "legitimate and overriding business consideration" provides justification. The Courts will balance these "justifications" against the countervailing national interest in eliminating employment discrimination. It is important for management to remember the Supreme Court's admonishment to employers:

> "...practices and procedures, or tests, neutral on their face, and even neutral in terms of intent, cannot be maintained if they operate to freeze the status quo of prior discriminatory employment practices."

Even if the employer can show such an overriding business justification, the charging party still has one more chance. He or she can show that those reasons are merely a pretext for discrimination. Such evidence might include proof of past intentional discrimination, or proof that an alternative practice would serve your legitimate business interests with less disparate impact. Almost all disparate impact cases will have some statistical evidence showing the discriminatory impact on a particular protected class.

Although traditionally employees challenging internal promotion decisions had to use the disparate treatment analysis, the United States Supreme Court has held that employees may utilize the disparate impact analysis. The Supreme Court held the disparate impact analysis applicable to promotions to supervisory positions.

Remember: To apply a disparate impact analysis, the employee does not need to prove intent. The program challenged must be facially neutral and have an adverse impact on minorities.

Remember: Always have objective criteria established for promotions. Take out as much subjectivity as possible from the promotion procedure.

Remember: Keep an accurate applicant flow log detailing who applies for each job opening.

Disparate Treatment – *Prima Facie* Case

A somewhat different, but no less important (and the more prevalent), theory of discrimination is that two or more individuals have been treated differently (unfairly) strictly because one is in a protected class and the other is not. In order to establish a *prima facie* case under a disparate treatment theory, the plaintiff must show facts which support an inference of the employer's intent to discriminate. It is clear that a *prima facie* case may be made without direct proof of discriminatory motivation. After all, we know that a supervisor will not testify on the witness stand that he intentionally fired someone solely because that employee was Black, female, or Hispanic, etc.

The Courts will allow the charging party to make such a showing with a combination of direct, circumstantial and statistical evidence of discrimination. These facts give rise to a "presumption of discrimination." That is, if management doesn't disprove or otherwise explain the plaintiff's evidence then the Court will enter judgment for the plaintiff, because no issue of fact will remain.

Therefore, the burden shifts to the company to rebut the presumption of discrimination raised by the charging party by offering evidence that actions were non-discriminatory and legitimate. It is important to understand that the burden does not shift away from the plaintiff to prove its case. But, as in any case, employers must bring forth facts to rebut the plaintiff's case.

The employer needs only to produce admissible evidence which would allow the judge or jury to conclude rationally that the employment decision was not based on or motivated by discriminatory reasons.

The presentation of proof then shifts back to the plaintiff to show that the employer's stated reasons were not the true reason for the employment decision. The plaintiff can either persuade the judge that a discriminatory reason was the more likely reason for the action, or that the employer's reasons are simply not believable.

Although in many of these cases executives feel that they are "guilty until proven innocent," the plaintiff must still prove his or her case. The company must be prepared to defend its position by stating legitimate and non-discriminatory reasons for employment policies and decisions. This can only be done with a thorough in-house investigation of every facet of the case. Treat this internal investigation as if you were the judge or the EEOC investigator.

The Supreme Court decided that when a plaintiff in a Title VII case proves that her gender played a part in an employment decision, the defendant employer may avoid a finding of liability by proving by a preponderance of the evidence that it would have made the same decision even if it had not taken the plaintiff's gender into account. The Court held that any inquiry into the process requires looking at all of the reasons both legitimate and illegitimate, contributing to the decision *at the time* it is made. The preservation of the employer's freedom of choice means that the employer will not be liable if it can prove that, if it had not taken gender into account, it would have come to the same decision. The employer must always show, however, that it had a legitimate reason, which standing alone would have allowed the employer to terminate the employee (mixed motive).

The company need not prove that it made the right decision, only that the decision you made was not influenced by discriminatory factors. For example a Federal Court held where the company terminated a Black teller for dishonesty, and it was later determined that she was not guilty, as long as the company acted under a good faith belief that the teller was dishonest, there was not a violation of Title. VII. The company proved that race was not a factor in the termination, but those irregularities in the employee's cash drawer were the real reasons.

In the same vein, employers must investigate the situation and advance legitimate business reasons for their conduct. Just because the employee happens to be in a protected class does not mean that the company is guilty of anything. However, be objective in the internal investigation. See it from both sides. The following section provides guidance for your investigation.

After Acquired Evidence

This concept is very helpful to employers. If you find out information **after** the employee is terminated that would have led you to terminate that person had you known of the information while the employee was employed by you, you may use this as a defense to limit the employee's damages. So in a discrimination discharge case, if you can prove that after the employee left, you found evidence of stealing, your defense is that had you known at the time of the theft, you would have terminated the employee. That certainly limits the back pay that the employee is seeking.

Internal Procedures

Thorough Investigation

First and foremost, the employer must conduct a thorough investigation of the allegation. If the charge by the aggrieved party is unclear, then management should seek clarification of the allegation. Remember, the employer cannot prepare for an investigation if it is not certain what it is preparing against. Once the nature of the charge is understood, gather all facts which support the particular action, conduct or episode which resulted in the allegation of discrimination. Review all documentation that would be pertinent to the particular matter. If any document contains damaging information or permits inferences adverse to the company's position, attempt to find out about it and be prepared to give an explanation for it.

Interview all witnesses who have information regarding the episode, event or conduct and document these interviews. Preferably, get these employees to read the notes to ensure that they are an accurate transcription of what was said and have them sign them. Review all other information such as employee files, work rules and policies. Similarly, if any statements by employees are made which give a negative inference, be certain to investigate in order to be able to respond to these negative inferences.

Review Merits of Charge

After having completed a thorough investigation of all the facts and documentation regarding the allegation, it is essential to determine objectively whether a strong case exists to support the conduct, practice or policy that resulted in the charge of discrimination. In this decision-making process, it is also imperative to consider whether the individual charge could balloon into a class action should an investigation be conducted. In other words, although the investigator comes in initially under an individual charge, upon observation of records and testimony of witnesses, he or she could enlarge the individual action into a class action which could result in substantial damages. If the decision is reached after a thorough investigation and analysis that your case is weak, it would be best to consider the pre-determination settlement discussed later.

Prepare Position Statement

A position statement is imperative if the employer is going to prevail. A position statement is a summation of the facts in issue as the employer sees them and the company's position and authority for its position. The advantage of preparing a position statement is that the charging party is unlikely to be represented by an attorney so will issue no such statement. The investigator is typically too busy to do sufficient research to investigate the legal issues involved. Since the advantage is with the employer in this instance, it is necessary to formulate the facts as they are seen by the employer and to demonstrate by legal authority why the company's position is not discriminatory. Since, typically, the investigator's only source of legal information regarding the issue is the company's position statement, it carries substantially more weight in the decision rendered by the investigator.

Regarding the position statement, however, it is important that it reflect an accurate account of the practice, program or event which resulted in the charge of discrimination. This is necessary since this position statement must be relied on by the company in further proceedings.

Retaliation

The U.S. Supreme Court ruled that retaliating against an employee who has participated in an **internal investigation** is illegal conduct. So be sure that after you have completed your internal investigation, no witness or participant in the investigation becomes the victim of discrimination/retaliation. Further, the Supreme Court in another case held that it is also illegal retaliation to discipline a "significant other" or spouse in order to get back at an employee who has filed a discrimination complaint. If you know that employees are co-habiting or married, take steps to prevent any adverse action against the non-charging partner. As a general rule, the Employee must prove "but for" the protected EEOC activity, he/she would not have been fired (or in other ways retaliated against).

How to Deal with the EEOC and OFCCP

Critical Points to Remember when Dealing with the EEOC (or your local agency) in the Event of a Charge

- Any charge has the potential of winding up as a class action. As a result of this fact, it is imperative that the employer investigate thoroughly every allegation and, where possible, narrow the investigation down to those specific allegations as set out in the charging party's complaint.
- Anything you willingly furnish the agency in the beginning will be available against you throughout the case. As such, it is important that the information provided and statements made are an accurate reflection of what occurred. Further, the decision to provide information and documentation willingly should not be made without first doing a thorough investigation and feeling assured that the company's case is a strong one.
- At the outset, the employer should get a concise statement from the government of how it views the case. This is especially significant because it is often likely for the charging party to make an allegation which will be ambiguous. If

this is so, it will be difficult to investigate. Therefore, the employer should know absolutely what has been alleged to be discriminatory.

- Limit EEOC interviewing of employees. There is no obligation on the employer's part to allow the EEOC or state Fair Employment Practices (FEP) agencies to come in and interview employees on company time. However, as a show of good faith, it is normally a good practice to provide this time. Before such interviews take place, it is imperative for the employer to inter-view the employees to know what they are going to say and to instruct them not to volunteer any information that hasn't been requested by the investigator. The wit-ness should be instructed to answer only the questions that have been posed by the investigator and to answer them truthfully.

- Insist the EEOC demonstrate relevancy before disclosing documents such as an affirmative action program. This is critical since the EEOC or other state FEP agency may come in and request as much documentation as possible to develop a general pattern or practice of discriminatory conduct despite the fact that the allegation is limited to a narrow charge of individual discrimination. What makes this fact so important is that should an investigator come in and investigate on an individual charge and yet be furnished information sufficient to prove a "pattern and practice" type of charge, then such charge will ensue and the employer may be liable for it rather than just an indi-vidual charge.

Dealing with the OFCCP during an Investigation

Obtain a complete list of all deficiencies in writing before beginning negotiations or making meaningful concessions. It is likely that the OFCCP will continue to revise its list of possible violations and therefore, require the employer to concede to further demands. To avoid this situation, be certain that the list of deficiencies initially provided is in writing and secure from the OFCCP the fact that the list is final.

Attempt to get a letter of commitment rather than conciliation agreement. As with the EEOC, it is always preferable to get a letter of commitment rather than a conciliation agreement as the conciliation agreement is far more formal and therefore will serve as a red flag to the OFCCP or EEOC in future investigations of discrimination against the employer.

Do not allow open-ended conciliatory agreement. Ensure that a time limit is set. The standard conciliation agreement provides for OFCCP compliance to remain in full force and effect until such time as the agency finds the contractor to have met all the terms of this agreement. This open-ended agreement is highly unacceptable to the employer and would impose a substantial burden upon the company at the whim of the OFCCP.

Be certain that all goals and timetables agreed to in conciliation are reasonable. Do not be bullied into agreeing to specific goals and timetables as set out by the OFCCP. If, based on the employer's research, it is unlikely that the government goals and timetables are reasonable, challenge them and counter-propose the company's own set of goals and timetables.

Do not concede to back pay as a result of agency statistics–disprove where possible through alternate statistics.

Alternate Time Frames

Establish defensible criteria, *i.e.*, content, valid job qualifications, evaluate applicant flow separately for those who meet criteria and those who do not.

The On-Site Investigation

It is extremely important that all appropriate departments have knowledge of the particular allegation. For instance, it is possible that the charge will go to a plant manager, when it should have been sent initially to an HR or legal department. Be certain that every department that should have knowledge of the charge receives it in sufficient time to participate in the investigation and decision-making process.

Before the investigator comes on-site to conduct his or her investigation, be sure it is known what the witnesses say. They should be informed not to volunteer information to the investigator, but only to answer the questions truthfully.

When the investigator arrives, it is important to be friendly at all times. There will be no advantage to arguing with the investigator or complaining about the unfairness of the charge. It is critical to understand that the investigator's job is to look for evidence of discrimination and it is the company's job to show legitimate business reasons.

Unless the case the company has is exceptionally strong, it is best not to state the company case but rather to allow the investigator to ask the questions that he or she needs to ask to develop his or her case. One exception to this rule would be if the investigator asks a question and it is answered by the witness in a partial fashion. In that situation, the employer, or its representative, should ask sufficient questions to clarify the matter and put it in the best light for the employer.

Although it is typically a practice for the investigator to request that affidavits be prepared, or, in other words, that the witnesses sign a sworn statement, it is advised that no such affidavit be signed. The law does not obligate the witnesses or the employer to sign the sworn affidavit. The advantage of not signing sworn affidavits is that such affidavits can be used in rebuttal to any testimony presented at a later date and there is no advantage for the employer to be confined to these statements which could later be used to discredit the witnesses' testimony.

The employer should not provide any documentation to the investigator unless specifically requested or unless the documentation is strongly in favor of the company's position. Typically, however, the agency will be able to secure what documentation it needs through its subpoena powers.

Another managerial employee or representative of the company should always be present during an investigation and that individual should be taking copious notes to ensure that what has been said and what the investigator documents is accurate.

Finally, it is essential that the company attempt to keep the investigator within the narrow confines of the allegation. It is not unlikely for the investigator to stray from the allegation and wind up talking about sex discrimination when the initial charge was race discrimination. Should the investigator be allowed to accomplish this task, it is likely that the resulting charge will be more than the initial allegation that the charging party filed.

The company does have the right, and should insist on it, to be present when management employees are being interviewed. However, no such right exists as to non-management employees. That is why it is important to interview these employees before the investigator arrives.

Considering Settlement

Consider:
- Cost Standpoint
- Class Action Standpoint
- Viable Position Standpoint

Better to Defend Now if Viable Case

Consider:
- Dollar factor
- Dissuades charging party from taking further action
- Requests for consideration by EEOC not granted
- Court will use agency decision as evidence against (or for) you
- Where no probable cause found, EEOC generally rubber-stamps

The Fact-Finding Conference

Most state and local Fair Employment Practices (FEP) agencies have a fact-finding conference instead of an on-site investigation. This conference takes place in the agency's office and is usually preceded by the agency's request that the employer bring certain documents and witnesses.

Prior to the conference, send the investigator all the requested information and a detailed position statement as to why the company has not committed a discriminatory act.

The conference is conducted by the investigator and executives will be asked questions concerning their conduct. This is the opportunity to make a major impact on how the decision will go. Bring every conceivable piece of documentation that supports the company's position. Bring witnesses to buttress the documentation.

This will be the best opportunity to rebut the charging party's claims. Make the most of it!

After the charging party presents his or her side, the employer will usually be allowed to ask him or her questions. Typically, this is done through the investigator. That is, your representative asks the investigator to ask the charging party the question. This prevents crosstalk and arguments between the two sides. The conference goes faster and more is accomplished without the bickering and bantering in which some employees like to engage.

Sometimes after the fact-finding conference the employer will get requests for more information. More commonly, however, if your job was done thoroughly, the next correspondence received should be the agency's findings in your favor!

Conciliation and the Public Hearing

A. Conciliation Settlement

Let's assume that the company has now gone through the investigation, the fact-finding conference and has received a finding of cause against it.

At that point the agency will attempt to settle the matter through conciliation without calling the employer into a public hearing. It is at this point where management must consider whether or not there is any common ground upon which it and the charging party can agree. If not, go to the public hearing. If so, review the pros and cons of the settlement.

> Remember: Once the company makes a bona fide offer of reinstatement, its back pay liability stops at that point.

B. The Public Hearing

Should conciliation fail, the employer will be called to a public hearing. At this state, a lawyer's services are indispensable. Why? Because any appeal that is taken is usually reviewed by the Appellate court on the record made at the public administrative hearing. If the record made doesn't support the company's position, the chances of winning on appeal are slim and none.

Therefore, the attorney must prepare the case as though it were a full trial in federal court. He/she should send interrogatories, requests for admissions and production of documents, take depositions, and any other actions deemed pertinent, if allowed. In short, he/she should use every pretrial tactic he/she can to get all the information about the other side's case.

The actual hearing is like a trial where the rules of evidence, although applicable, are usually loosely followed by the hearing officer. It is important for the lawyer to create a good record, present the evidence in a logical manner and not leave out crucial elements of a defense to a prima facie case that the courts look to in order to find for the company.

Difference between Consent Decree and Settlement

Consent decrees and settlement agreements are favored means of providing relief from employment discrimination. They are mechanisms used by the EEOC to bring Title VII litigants or potential litigants to a mutual agreement concerning both the necessary and proper relief to be provided and the terms under which the relief will be granted.

The consent decree is a formal instrument that has court approval from its outset and thus a violation of it can result in contempt of court.

A settlement agreement may occasionally be informal such as a letter of agreement between the parties.

The subject matter of a consent decree or settlement agreement will cover the facts and circumstances of the case. The decree or agreement may cover all substantive action which is generally the subject of Title VII relief, including but not limited to hiring, reinstatement, promotion, alteration of discriminatory employment practices, guarantees of future nondiscriminatory policies, affirmative action plans, retroactive wage or pension adjustments and back pay awards.

Remember: Where possible, the company is advised to seek a settlement agreement rather than a consent decree as the consent decree will put it under the control of the court and result in contempt should a violation be found.

Choosing an Attorney

The first question the company must decide is the need for an attorney to represent it. If so, at what stage can he or she do the most good?

If there are experienced personnel who have knowledge in the EEO area and who are familiar with what it takes to defend a charge, the employer may not need an attorney at all unless or until it is called into a public hearing (after a finding of cause against it).

However, favorable results are generally based on an in-depth investigation and solid preparation by an attorney who is experienced and knowledgeable in the equal employment opportunity field. Not only is the area of law familiar, but so are the processes the agency uses, the investigator's requirements and idiosyncrasies.

For example, recently an employer was called in for a fact-finding conference which was to last approximately three hours or so. Before the conference began, the investigator took the attorney aside and asked him what he really thought about the merits of that case. He told her candidly that this employer was not guilty and why. She went to speak to the charging party and within half an hour the matter was settled for a neutral letter of reference given to the employee. This saved considerable time (and attorneys' fees) and management time (the president of the company and his human resources manager were the witnesses) and made the client happy.

How was this accomplished? It was done quickly because the attorney had worked with the agency and the investigators frequently. He knew how to approach the person with the facts, and had built a rapport with the investigators. They respected his analysis. Here is the greatest benefit an experienced attorney can have. They know the people and can prepare the case with an eye toward the particular agency, investigator or hearing officer involved.

Management can also choose an expert from outside its area. The benefit of this is that the experienced counsel can lend a fresh approach and influence to the situation. No matter where the lawyer comes from, he/she must be thoroughly familiar with this area of the law. It will not do to have a tax lawyer, a corporate attorney or the estate law expert represent your company. Unless they do this every day, they will have to educate themselves in this area of the law, which is becoming highly specialized and technical. This will increase the costs.

Beware of the experts who tell you they can win them all or that "we'll fight this one all the way to the Supreme Court." Statements of this type show a decided lack of understanding of the delicate process of negotiation and persuasion that is necessary when dealing with EEO agencies. If the company's attorney takes the hardline approach in every case no matter what, the employer may spend literally thousands of dollars defending a charge that could have been settled amicably and with little cost to it in dollars or lost pride.

In any event, the choice of when to hire the attorney is critical. It is recommended an attorney be hired in the beginning where he or she may defuse the situation quickly. However, if the HR department is knowledgeable and experienced in this area, there is no reason why it can't do the job until management needs the legal expertise for a public hearing.

Attorneys' Fees

Win or lose, one aspect of EEO litigation that every company must consider is the cost of attorneys' fees. This means the plaintiff's attorneys fees as well as its own. Section 2000e 5(k) of Title 42 of the U.S. Code provides in part that in an action brought under Title VII ."..The Court in its discretion may allow the prevailing party ...a reasonable attorney fee." In a case that began in an administrative proceeding, progressing through years of litigation, a simple non-class action suit could generate $20,000 to $50,000 in attorneys' fees.

If the employee is ultimately successful, the defendant will pay that person's attorneys' fees, regardless of the actual amount the company pays the plaintiff in damages. The Courts have decided that they will review the issues of the case, determine on which issues the claimant "prevailed" or was successful, and then award attorneys' fees for the time spent prosecuting those claims. No award will be made for unsuccessful claims unless those failed issues were necessary to the suit as a whole. If the plaintiff enters into a settlement with the company, to dispose of all the issues in the case the separate matter of the attorneys' fees will also be settled unless they are specifically reserved for later resolution.

In a Federal Circuit race discrimination case, the plaintiff settled his case for $3,000. The attorney then made an application for $24,000 in attorneys' fees. The Court held that because attorneys' fees were a disputed issue and all disputed issues were settled by the settlement agreement, the attorney was not entitled to a fee from the defendant.

However, the Supreme Court of the United States has said that the attorney fee issue is separate from the issues of the lawsuit. In essence, the Court is saying that a request for attorneys' fees is not necessarily subsumed by a decision on the merits of the case Therefore, it is extremely important that whenever an employer enters into a settlement with the plaintiff at either the administrative or court stage a specific reference to attorneys' fees must be made. In fact, the plaintiff's attorney should sign a release of his claims too. Then there is no question remaining.

What if the state your company is in doesn't allow attorneys' fees to be granted to a prevailing plaintiff in state EEO litigation? You must still be concerned, because the U.S. Supreme Court has held that the federal courts may grant attorneys' fees for the services of the plaintiffs' attorney in state administrative proceeding. It is therefore, incumbent that even if the case hasn't gone to trial or been filed in federal court, any settlement entered into contains a release from liability of the plaintiff's attorneys' fees.

The Courts do also grant attorneys' fees to the prevailing defendant. Although the standard for the employer to obtain its attorneys' fees from the plaintiff are different than the plaintiffs, some defendants have been awarded their attorneys' fees. In many instances, however, this is a hollow victory because of the inability of the employer to collect from the plaintiff. In any event, it serves to set an example to others that they should not file frivolous claims just to collect "nuisance value" settlements.

The U.S. Supreme Court stated that a defendant will only be granted its attorneys' fees under the following standards:

A plaintiff shall not be assessed his opponent's attorneys' fees unless a court finds his claim was frivolous, unreasonable or groundless, or that the plaintiff continued to litigate after it clearly became so. And, needless to say, if a plaintiff is found to have brought or continued such a claim in bad faith, there will be an even stronger basis for charging him the attorneys' fees incurred by the defense.

In summary, one of the biggest costs in any lawsuit will be your own attorneys' fees. If the company is also assessed the plaintiffs attorneys' fees, the employer could be obligated to pay an inordinately large amount. This may enter into the analysis of when and whether the company wants to settle. As a strategy, management may wish to offer a reasonable settlement which it feels the plaintiff will take. This puts the plaintiff's attorney in the dilemma of advising his or her client to turn down a good settlement offer, which the Court will review when it comes time to review his attorneys' fees, or advising the client to take a settlement which is good for the client, but bad for the attorney.

Any pressure the defendant can put on the plaintiff or his or her attorney is important.

Employment at Will and Unjust Dismissal or Whatever Happened to: "I can fire anyone for any reason"?

It seems clear that the old concept of the employer being able to terminate (fire) an employee at any time for any reason or no reason at all (the "at will" doctrine) is quickly being eroded. In some states, the common law doctrine of firing anyone at will is gone entirely. For example, South Dakota and Arkansas already have statutes placing the burden of proof on the employer to show that the firing of an employee must be for either habitual neglect of duty, continued incapacity to perform, or willful breach of duty. Many courts (as opposed to state legislatures) are doing away with the entire concept for a variety of reasons. For instance, unlawful discharge was found in the following cases:

1. Termination for an employee's refusal to participate in illegal activities or reporting those activities to the authorities. This is "whistle-blowing" and many states have laws against discharging employees for reporting law violations.
2. Refusal to commit perjury.
3. Filling a worker's compensation claim.
4. Serving on a jury.
5. Refusing to take a polygraph test.
6. Using an attorney to negotiate an employment contract.
7. Preventing an employee from investing under the company's pension plan.
8. Violation of express or implied public policies, ethical principles or statutory mandates.
9. Breach of the company's personnel policies or handbooks.
10. Forcing a dump truck operator to drive a dump truck with known defective brakes.

The damages can be substantial. Jury verdicts in wrongful discharge cases have only increased over the years. Plaintiffs utilize mainly two theories under which to seek damages: tort and contract. In a case which made newspaper headlines and was the subject of a television documentary, the jury awarded $2.3 million, including $467,000 in attorneys' fees. Much of this award was back pay and front pay under age discrimination. But also the jury gave the three employees money for their pain, suffering and emotional distress.

A Michigan jury awarded a man $450,000 who was discharged for filing a worker's compensation claim. In Oregon, the jury came in with a verdict of $125,000 in favor of a sales clerk where the department store in which she worked coerced her to sign a confession for theft and then told people that she was fired for stealing.

"Extreme and outrageous" conduct was how the court characterized the company's conduct in another case. Here the employer began terminating employees alphabetically in order to obtain information on thefts. Naturally, this conduct gave rise to damages for emotional distress.

Of course, not all employer conduct will give rise to damages. Not all courts will emasculate the "at will" doctrine so completely. One court refused to allow an action for intentional infliction of emotional distress unless the employer's conduct surrounding the discharge is so outrageous "as to go beyond all possible bounds of decency."

Finally, even where a possible Title VII discrimination case may be thrown out, the employer may still face the contract, tort and public policy problems discussed in the following pages.

Where an employee's sexual harassment Title VII claim was filed too late, a federal appeals court said she could still attempt to prove wrongful discharge under an implied covenant of good faith and fair dealing. Further, she could also attempt to prove that her supervisor (and the company) had intentionally inflicted emotional distress on her.

Privacy

Employees can also sue their employers for a violation of their right to privacy under many state laws. This means that an employer has, through its action, violated an employee's right to privacy, either to be free from illegal search and seizure or to be free from intrusion into their home life or the like. Thus, employers are well advised to remember that they should be extremely careful in dealing with the employee's private life and in fact their business life. Statistics for employees have gotten somewhat better in the last 40 years, but the amounts have gone up!

> *Remember:* You may be sued for common law claims even though you may win the Title VII action.

Tort Theory

In these cases the plaintiffs seek damages for intentional infliction of emotional distress, pain and suffering. Courts have in the past been reluctant to award damages, but now even the most conservative judges are allowing these cases to go to the jury. And of course juries can be a great equalizer to the plaintiff. If the employee's case isn't dismissed by the judge, the employee can expect a jury to award him/her substantial damages. Why? Because many employees (jurors) see the defendant employer as the employer they once had, who caused, or is causing them emotional distress. Therefore, an employer will be facing an uphill battle if it has truly treated the employee unfairly.

Contract Theory

Damages are sought for breach of the contract of employment. Implicit in all this is what courts have termed a "covenant of good faith and fair dealing." This means that the employer must treat its employees fairly and justly. If it fails to do so, it has breached an implied condition of the "employment" contract." Some states such as Arizona have made the employment relationship contractual by statute.

Not all courts today have adopted this exception to the "at will" doctrine. They hold that an agreement to give employment, even an agreement to give permanent employment, simply means to give a steady job of some permanence, as opposed to temporary or seasonal employment. To carry this one step farther, the courts have generally held that in the absence of some further implied or express stipulation as to the duration of the employment or of a good consideration in addition to (something other than) the services contracted for, the employment relationship is no more than a general hiring, terminable at will.

The Supreme Court of California held that a wrongful discharge claim for a breach of an implied covenant of good faith and fair dealing, can give rise to a contract action. However, the Court said that the plaintiff cannot have tort damages (e.g., pain and suffering, emotional distress, etc.) The significance of this case, however, is that the Court held that a contract can be formed by reviewing the "totality of the circumstances," and that there is no limitation for bringing this action. This is an important case because it is a victory for employees in the sense that they do have a cause of action for breach of contract, but do not have to show that an actual contract was entered into between the parties. It is also a win for employers because it limits the amount of damages that can be obtained by a prevailing plaintiff to contract damages, e.g., lost wages, lost benefits, etc.

Yet, having said all that, courts are willing in many instances to get around that position and rule in favor of the plaintiff. If the plaintiff can show malice or bad faith by the employer, the courts are more willing to find that the contractual relationship existed and was breached.

Handbooks

The use of employee handbooks by companies is widespread. Little does management know that lurking between the covers of the personnel manual, handbook, policy manual, etc., lurks a possible contract. The courts are beginning to hold that where the employee relied on the handbook or personnel policy in accepting the employment, failure of the company to follow its own rules will be a breach of contract.

It is imperative that during the hiring process the prospective employee not be given a copy of the handbook. Also, management should not get into the inner workings of the human resources system, such as a grievance procedure or the fact that termination will only result by willful acts or for cause.

In all instances, handbooks or policy manuals given to employees should have in writing a disclaimer stating that it is not a contract and should not be construed as such. Courts have that changed the character of the handbook from a contract to a "unilateral expression of policy end procedures," the terms of which are not bargained for. Further, these same courts hold that benefits conferred were "mere gratuities."

Management must make it clear to all employees that the handbook merely states certain benefits (*i.e.*, grievance procedure, pensions, health and life insurance) that are given to the employees voluntarily by the company. Because of this, they can be taken away. The company handbook is one of the areas where a company can be most vulnerable to a challenge to the "at will" doctrine.

Public Policy

The final exception being carved out by the courts is the public policy exception. This includes the "whistleblower" cases wherein employees report some wrongdoing of the employer. Courts hold that it is against public policy to allow an employer to fire someone for this reason. Several states have enacted "whistleblower" statutes. (*i.e.*, Connecticut, Michigan, Nebraska, Washington, New York.)

Where the employee is fired because he or she is attempting to encourage the employer to follow the law, courts have allowed a cause of action. Again, the theory is that it would be contrary to public policy to allow an employer to fire someone who is attempting to get the employer to follow the law.

The general concept is that where the firing violates a clear mandate of public policy, liability will result. This "clear mandate" is expressed either in a statute, regulation, or court case.

I represented an employee who was driving a heavily loaded dump truck. He ran a stop sign because of defective brakes. Luckily no one was injured, but the Department of Transportation refused to allow it to be moved until it had "field repairs" to the brakes. These were done to the limited extent that the truck could be driven back to the shop. Before any real repairs were made, the employer demanded that my client drive the truck to a job site over 30 miles away. When he refused, he was fired. There was a statute on the books that made it illegal to drive a motor vehicle with defective brakes. We won the case and indeed made some precedent setting law. The court held that firing someone in this instance violated the public policy of the state, because the employer could not punish someone for refusing to violate the motor vehicle laws.

Remember: As further examples of protected conduct, if an employee calls the Occupational Safety and Health Administration (OSHA), files a workers' compensation claim, or calls the labor department for a pay violation, do not terminate the employee for this reason. If you do, you will surely run up against the "public policy" exception to the "at will" doctrine if the employee sues.

Protect Yourself

Here is a list of things management can do to protect the company and its supervisors from liability. Remember though, that any employee can sue you at any time for any reason. However, these preventive measures may more likely make you a winner if you should get sued.

    A. Never promise any applicant for employment a permanent job. Never say "you've got a job here as long as you want it;" or "nobody ever gets fired around here;" or "as

long as you do your job, you have a job here for life."
These statements can lead to the implication of a contract
of employment.

B. Remove all references to permanent employment, termination for just cause, probationary periods, etc., from your handbook or policy manual. Everyone should always be on probation. The probationary period should be abolished because upon expiration of the probationary period, you may have to show cause for termination.

Put this disclaimer in your handbook:

"This handbook is not a contract, but is merely a statement of benefits the company is granting voluntarily. This handbook creates no contractual rights and all employment is 'at will.' Employees may be terminated with or without cause at any time, and employees may leave the company at any time."

C. Be consistent in the application of your policies. Once you grant severance pay or an extra sick day to one employee, you may have created a contract to do so with all employees. Don't place your company in that position. Have a benefit or a policy and stick to it!

D. A strong training program is essential for your managers and supervisors. Train them in what to say and what not to say in an interview or when dealing with employees. If you can't afford outside consultants or lawyers to train your people, buy inexpensive video training or handbooks. The cost you pay will be well worth the money you save and you will have the additional benefit of increased employee morale.

E. Documentation of the employee files is essential to a solid and winning defense. Have some type of progressive discipline procedure whereby documentation is generated. No case can be won where the employee's performance appraisals show that he or she "walks on water." Document the discipline and have a system which is uniformly applied to all.

F. The application form you use should state directly over the signature: "<u>I understand that if I am hired, the employment shall be at the will of either party and may be terminated by either party at any time.</u>"

G. Never discuss an employee's termination from employment. First, it's nobody's business, and second, it will lead to hard feelings on the part of the fired employee. This in turn leads to lawsuits and discrimination charges for invasion of privacy, defamation, or infliction of intentional distress.

H. Protect yourself against whistleblowers who use that as a means to get at the company. Institute a policy whereby the employee is required to report all law violations to management before going to an agency so that the company can correct the problem first. In this way, if he or she does not the company may fire the employee for not following its policies, which is legitimate.

I. If you believe the employee has a potential claim, offer a written termination agreement which prevents him or her from suing you in exchange for severance benefits.

J. Never give written reasons for your termination unless your state law requires it be done (as in Missouri; Mo Ann. Stat. §290.140 requires letter with reasons upon request). Choose your words at termination carefully. Statements such as "we need a younger image," or "you just don't fit," can cause a discrimination charge.

<u>Remember</u>: You must not apply these suggestions mechanically. Use the ones that work for your company. Do not increase management-employee tensions by using these ideas if they don't fit. Used improperly, they can backfire and cause more psychological and legal problems. The best advice is to use good judgment and solid management techniques to prevent the problems from arising.

Immigration Reform and Control Act
Employment Procedures Required

The Immigration Reform and Control Act of 1986 (IRCA) affects all employers ranging from the individual hiring domestic help to large corporations. The law prohibits the hiring of illegal aliens after November 6, 1986 and imposes sanctions on employers who fail to comply. Employers must follow these procedures:

1. Hire only citizens and aliens lawfully authorized to work in the United States.
2. Advise all job applicants of the employer's policy to such effect.
3. Within three business days after hire, require new employees to complete and sign Form I-9 (Employment Eligibility Verification) to certify that they are eligible for employment.
4. Examine documentation presented by new employees, record information about the documents on Form I-9, and sign the form.
5. Retain the form for three years or for one year past the end of employment of the individual, whichever is longer.
6. If requested, present Form I-9 for inspection by Homeland Security or Department of Labor officers. No reporting is required.

Verification of Work Status

Employers must ask all new hires for proof of identity and eligibility for employment. There are certain documents which can be used to establish both proof of identity and work authorization, for example, a U.S. passport, Certificate of U.S. Citizenship or Certificate of Naturalization. There are also approved documents which can be used to separately establish identity and work authorization. The most common combination: a driver's license plus Social Security card.

Failure to ask a new employee for verification of work status will subject employers to civil penalties which range from

$100 to $1,000, even if the person hired is a United States citizen. Employers are required to sign Form I-9 verifying that they asked for and were shown the necessary work authorization documents. In addition, each person hired must sign the same form verifying his or her eligibility to work in the United States.

Employer Penalties

The law applies only to illegal aliens hired after November 6, 1986.

An employer found by Homeland Security to have violated the Act is subject to an injunction against the illegal activity and to civil or criminal penalties. A first violation on or after June 1, 1988 will subject the violator to civil fines ranging from $250 to $2,000 for each unauthorized alien involved in the violation. Penalties for a second violation can run up to $10,000 for each illegal worker involved.

In addition, the regulations specify that "pattern and practice" violations are punishable by criminal fines of up to $2,000 for each violation, imprisonment of up to six months, or both.

Non-Discrimination Provision

The law makes it illegal to discriminate against legal aliens on the basis of citizenship status or national origin. The non-discrimination provisions were included in the law to prevent any bias in the employee selection that might result from the law's provisions sanctioning employers for hiring illegal aliens.

The law does not apply to employers with fewer than four employees. Employers with between four and 14 employees are covered by provisions prohibiting discrimination on the basis of citizenship and national origin. (Employers with fewer than fifteen employees fall outside of Title VII provisions forbidding discrimination based on national origin.) Employers with fifteen or more employees are subject to the law's provisions prohibiting discrimination on the basis of citizenship status.

Complaints of discrimination are investigated by a special counsel's office set up in the Justice Department. A finding of discrimination can result in fines up to $1,000 for each individual discriminated against.

Use of E-Verify

E-Verify is a computer-based system that allows the employer to check on the status of an employee by matching social security numbers. Some states mandate the use of e-verify. Check your state laws.

Concluding Thoughts

Now that you have an understanding of the law and have learned some techniques which should lessen the chance of discrimination complaints, I will give you my own subjective ideas about what you as a manager or supervisor must do and what is expected of you. But in the final analysis, if you treat your employees as you would want to be treated in the same circumstances, there is every likelihood that you can avoid a discrimination complaint.

Here then, are conclusions as to what is expected of you as a supervisor or manager.

1. Leave any personal prejudices of yours at the doorstep of your home. Failure to do so does your company a disservice.
2. Fully implement your company's equal employment opportunity policies.
3. Create and maintain the proper work atmosphere within your department and installation so that all employees are fully aware of your company's equal employment opportunity policies. There should be an absence of animosity or hard feelings between employee groups of any composition.
4. Be constantly alert and sensitive to possible inequalities of job assignments, opportunity, training, or any other aspect of employment.
5. Report to appropriate company management for review and corrective action, if necessary, any company policy,

practice or procedure which may act as a barrier to the full utilization of employees protected by the equal employment opportunity laws. Similarly, make any recommendations you think could aid the company's affirmative action program.

6. Make every effort to encourage and assist qualified employees from underutilized groups, such as racial minorities and females, to advance within your company. This would include encouraging their participation in training and educational programs, and providing career counseling when appropriate.

7. Do not tolerate prejudicial or discriminatory acts within your place of employment. One small incident can trigger a government inquiry or major court case. Report such acts immediately to appropriate company management. Racial or ethnic slurs or jokes can be offensive to certain groups and have no place in your place of employment.

8. Be considerate of your company's image in the minority community as well as the community at large, and strive to earn respect for your company through positive accomplishments in the area of equal employment.

Remember: Your Company must hold you accountable for meeting your equal employment opportunity responsibilities.

APPENDIX

SAMPLE POLICIES

Social Media Policy

At [Employer], we understand that social media can be a fun and rewarding way to share your life and opinions with family, friends and co-workers around the world. However, use of social media also presents certain risks and carries with it certain responsibilities. To assist you in making responsible decisions about your use of social media, we have established these guidelines for appropriate use of social media.

This policy applies to all associates who work for [Employer], or one of its subsidiary companies in the United States.

Managers and supervisors should use the supplemental Social Media Management Guidelines for additional guidance in administering the policy.

GUIDELINES

In the rapidly expanding world of electronic communication, *social media* can mean many things. *Social media* includes all means of communicating or posting information or content of any sort on the Internet, including to your own or someone else's web log or blog, journal or diary, personal web site, social networking or affinity web site, web bulletin board or a chat room, whether or not associated or affiliated with [Employer], as well as any other form of electronic communication.

The same principles and guidelines found in [Employer] policies and three basic beliefs apply to your activities online. Ultimately, you are solely responsible for what you post online. Before creating online content, consider some of the risks and rewards that are involved. Keep in mind that any of your conduct that adversely affects your job performance, the performance of fellow associates or otherwise adversely affects members, customers, suppliers, people who work on behalf of [Employer] or [Employer's] legitimate business interests may result in disciplinary action up to and including termination.

Know and follow the rules

Carefully read these guidelines, the [Employer] Statement of Ethics Policy, the [Employer] Information Policy and the Discrimination & Harassment Prevention Policy, and ensure your postings are consistent with these policies. Inappropriate postings that may include discriminatory remarks, harassment, and threats of violence or similar inappropriate or unlawful conduct will not be tolerated and may subject you to disciplinary action up to and including termination.

Be respectful

Always be fair and courteous to fellow associates, customers, members, suppliers or people who work on behalf of [Employer]. Also, keep in mind that you are more likely to resolve workrelated complaints by speaking directly with your co-workers or by utilizing our Open Door Policy than by posting complaints to a social media outlet. Nevertheless, if you decide to post complaints or criticism, avoid using statements, photographs, video or audio that reasonably could be viewed as malicious, obscene, threatening or intimidating, that disparage customers, members, associates or suppliers, or that might constitute harassment or bullying. Examples of such conduct might include offensive posts meant to intentionally harm someone's reputation or posts that could contribute to a hostile work environment on the basis of race, sex, disability, religion or any other status protected by law or company policy.

Be honest and accurate

Make sure you are always honest and accurate when posting information or news, and if you make a mistake, correct it quickly. Be open about any previous posts you have altered. Remember that the Internet archives almost everything; therefore, even deleted postings can be searched. Never post any information or rumors that you know to be false about [Employer], fellow associates, members, customers, suppliers, people working on behalf of [Employer] or competitors.

Post only appropriate and respectful content

- Maintain the confidentiality of [Employer] trade secrets and private or confidential information. Trade secrets may include information regarding the development of systems, processes, products, know-how and technology. Do not post internal reports, policies, procedures or other internal business-related confidential communications.
- Respect financial disclosure laws. It is illegal to communicate or give a "tip" on inside information to others so that they may buy or sell stocks or securities. Such online conduct may also violate the Insider Trading Policy.
- Do not create a link from your blog, website or other social networking site to [Employer] website without identifying yourself as a [Employer] associate.
- Express only your personal opinions. Never represent yourself as a spokesperson for [Employer]. If [Employer]

is a subject of the content you are creating, be clear and open about the fact that you are an associate and make it clear that your views do not represent those of [Employer], fellow associates, members, customers, suppliers or people working on behalf of [Employer]. If you do publish a blog or post online related to the work you do or subjects associated with [Employer], make it clear that you are not speaking on behalf of [Employer]. It is best to include a disclaimer such as "The postings on this site are my own and do not necessarily reflect the views of [Employer]."

Using social media at work

Refrain from using social media while on work time or on equipment we provide, unless it is work-related as authorized by your manager or consistent with the Company Equipment Policy. Do not use [Employer] e-mail addresses to register on social networks, blogs or other online tools utilized for personal use.

Retaliation is Prohibited

[Employer] prohibits taking negative action against any associate for reporting a possible deviation from this policy or for cooperating in an investigation. Any associate who retaliates against another associate for reporting a possible deviation from this policy or for cooperating in an investigation will be subject to disciplinary action, up to and including termination.

Media contacts

Associates should not speak to the media on [Employer's] behalf without contacting the Corporate Affairs Department. All media inquiries should be directed to them.

For more information

If you need further guidance, contact the Human Resources department.

Sexual Harassment Policy #1

Statement of Policy

It is the policy of (company name) that sexual harassment of its employees by anyone, whether management/supervisory personnel, fellow employees, or others, will not be tolerated. Such conduct will result in immediate disciplinary action including termination of employment.

Definition

Sexual harassment is defined as unwelcomed sexual advances of whatever nature, requests for sexual favors, or other verbal or physical conduct of a sexual nature when:

1. submission to such conduct is either an explicit or implicit condition of an individual's employment;
2. submission to, or rejection of, such conduct by an individual is used as the basis for employment decisions affecting such an individual, e.g., salary increase; or
3. such conduct has the purpose or effect of unreasonably interfering with an individual's work performance or creating an intimidating, hostile or offensive working environment.

Normally, courteous, mutually respectful, pleasant, non-coercive interactions between men women that are acceptable to both parties are not considered to be sexual harassment.

Responsibility

It is the responsibility of management personnel to insure a working environment free from sexual harassment and to make known to employees the policy of (company name) on sexual harassment. In addition, management is expected to take immediate action to deal promptly with known situations involving sexual harassment.

Complaint Procedure

1. An employee who believes he or she has been or is being subjected to sexual harassment should promptly notify his or her immediate supervisor. If the immediate supervisor is the person involved, the employee should notify that person's supervisor.
2. The supervisor who has received the notification is expected to immediately notify the Human Resources Office to which legal counsel is available. A coordinated effort will be commenced to investigate the complaint.
3. If the investigation validates the complaint, disciplinary action will be taken. Such action might range from counsel or warning to discharge, depending on the nature of the complaint and other factors.

Sexual Harassment and Other Unlawful Harassment Policy #2

Sexual harassment and discrimination at [Employer] is prohibited and is in violation of Federal and State law. It is the policy of [Employer] to provide a work environment free of harassment. As a preventative measure, this policy condemns contact that constitutes any form of harassment, including but not limited to racial, ethnic, religion, age, or sexual harassment, and [Employer] will take disciplinary measures, including termination, to ensure compliance with the policy set forth herein.

[Employer] will not tolerate conduct by any internal or external party that harasses, disrupts, or interferes with an employee's work performance or which creates an intimidating, offensive, or hostile environment. While all forms of harassment are prohibited, [Employer] wishes to emphasize that sexual harassment, including opposite-sex harassment and same-sex harassment, is specifically prohibited.

Definition of Sexual Harassment

Quid pro quo sexual harassment consists of unwelcome sexual advances, any request for sexual favors, and other verbal or physical conduct of a sexual nature when:

- Submission to such conduct is made explicitly or implicitly a term or condition of an individual's employment or participation in [Employer] sponsored activities; or
- Submission to or rejection of such conduct by an individual is used as the basis for decisions affecting such individual's employment or participation in [Employer] sponsored activities.

A **hostile work environment** is one in which unwelcome conduct of a sexual nature creates an uncomfortable work environment for some employees. A hostile environment includes such behaviors as sexual pictures, calendars, graffiti, obscene jokes, gestures, offensive language, comments about physical attributes, unwanted touching, leers, etc. Such conduct also includes the use of information systems (e-mail, internet, etc.) for the display or transmission of sexually explicit messages, images, or jokes. Any act that a reasonable person would find offensive is in violation of this policy.

Other illegal harassment and discrimination

[Employer] is committed to providing a work environment that is free of all other forms of illegal discrimination and unlawful harassment. Actions, words, jokes or comments based on an individual's race, color, religion, sex, national origin, age, disability, sexual preference or any other protected classification will not be tolerated.

Procedure

Each employee has a responsibility to maintain a workplace free from any form of sexual harassment and to report any complaints of harassment or discrimination. Any employee who believes that he/she has been subjected to sexual harassment or other forms of harassment/illegal discrimination by a supervisor, co-workers, visitors, vendors or patients must immediately report this to his/her supervisor. The supervisor must then immediately report the complaint to Human Resources. Employees also have the option to file a complaint directly with Human Resources or another management member.

[Employer] strictly prohibits retaliation against any employee for reporting allegations of harassment. Any employee who retaliates against an employee for coming forward with allegations of harassment will be disciplined up to and including discharge subsequent to the outcome of a separate investigation that indicates retaliation may have occurred. All complaints will be investigated promptly and will be handled confidentially to the extent reasonably possible in order to conduct an investigation. All employees are required to fully cooperate in any investigation.

Employees who report harassment will be notified of the outcome of the investigation. When the investigation indicates inappropriate conduct may have occurred, disciplinary action will be taken up to and including discharge. If the employee is not satisfied with the handling of a complaint or action taken, the employee must submit a written appeal to _____ within 10 working days from the date of notification of the investigation results. The decision of _____ is final.

Sexual Harassment Policy #3

It is the policy of (company name) to operate in a work environment free of conduct that can be construed as sexual harassment. To this end, the company will make every effort to follow the government regulations on sexual harassment. To live up to these regulations and to maintain a work environment free of sexual harassment, we will adhere to the following policy:

The law defines sexual harassment as follows:

Unwelcomed sexual advances, requests for sexual favors and other verbal or physical conduct of a sexual nature constitute sexual harassment when:

1. submission to such conduct is either an explicit or implicit condition of an individual's employment;
2. submission to, or rejection of, such conduct by an individual is used as the basis for employment decisions affecting such an individual, e.g., salary increase; or
3. such conduct has the purpose or effect of unreasonably interfering with an individual's work performance or creating an intimidating, hostile or offensive working environment.

All of the above are forbidden to take place between associates of (company name) on or off the job. Consensual relationships between associates that do not encompass the above prohibitions do not fall within the policy.

This policy is written to be sure everyone understands our intention to abide by this and other valid equal employment opportunity rules and regulations. Obviously, nothing can or will be done unless someone in management observes or is told about violations of this policy.

If you feel you are presently or in the future imposed upon, you should go to your supervisor immediately. If for some reason you do not get investigation and results, or you think your supervisor is part of the problem, go to the General Manager of the company.

Keep in mind that unless you give us the relevant facts promptly, we may not be able to help you to the maximum. Where the evidence is clear that someone is guilty, he or she will be dealt with promptly. The exact punishment will be determined by the seriousness of the offense, whether repeated, provable and other relevant facts.

In all cases, we will try to treat all associates in similar situations in the same even-handed manner.

Should a complaint be registered by an associate against another, the person complained against must give full disclosure of all relevant facts, as does the complaining person. There will be no retaliation against any associate for the bringing to the attention of management any incident of sexual harassment.

A copy of the EEOC's regulations on sexual harassment follows.

Part 1604 – Guidelines on Discrimination Because of Sex

A. Harassment on the basis of sex is a violation of Sec. 703 of Title VII. Unwelcome sexual advances, requests for sexual favors, and other verbal or physical conduct of a sexual nature constitute sexual harassment when:

1. submission to such conduct is made either explicitly or implicitly a term of an individual's employment;
2. submission to or rejection of such conduct by an individual is used as the basis for employment decisions affecting such individual; or
3. such conduct has the purpose or effect of unreasonably interfering with an individual's work performance or creating an intimidating, hostile or offensive working environment.

B. In determining whether alleged conduct constitutes sexual harassment, the commission will look at the record as a whole and at the totality of the circumstances, such as the nature of the sexual advances and the context which the alleged incidents occurred. The determination of the legality of a particular action will be made from the facts, on a case by case basis.

C. Applying general Title VII principles, an employer, employment agency joint apprenticeship committee or labor organization (hereinafter collectively referred to as "employer") is responsible for its acts and those of its agents and supervisory employees with respect to sexual harassment regardless of whether the specific acts complained of were authorized or even forbidden by the employer and regardless of whether the employer knows or should have known of their occurrence. The Commission will examine the circumstances of the particular employment relationship and the job functions performed by the individual in determining whether an individual acts in either a supervisory or agency capacity.

D. With respect to persons other than those mentioned in paragraph (c) of this section, an employer is responsible for acts of sexual harassment in the workplace where the employer, or its agents or supervisory employee, knows or should have known of the conduct. An employer may rebut apparent liability for such acts by showing that it took immediate and appropriate corrective action.

E. Prevention is the best tool for the elimination of sexual harassment. An employer should take steps necessary to prevent sexual harassment from occurring, such as affirmatively raising the subject, expressing strong disapproval, developing appropriate sanctions, informing employees of their right to raise and have to raise the issue of harassment under Title VII, and developing methods to sensitize all concerned.

Any employee who feels that he or she is a victim of sexual harassment should immediately report the matter to _____. Violations of this policy will not be permitted and may result in discipline up to and including discharge.

Sample Sexual Harassment Policy for Supervisors

It is the company's policy to prohibit harassment of one employee by another on the basis of sex. The purpose of this policy is not to regulate our employees' personal morality. It is to assure that, in the workplace, no employee harasses another on the basis of sex. While it is not easy to define precisely what harassment is, it certainly includes unwelcome sexual advances, requests for sexual favors and other verbal or physical conduct of a sexual nature such as uninvited touching or sexually related comments.

All members of management should be advised of this policy and held accountable for the effective administration of its intent throughout their respective organizations. Should a manager or supervisor be advised of an infraction of this policy, he/she should immediately report the incident to _____.

Violations of this policy should not be permitted and may result in discipline up to and including discharge.

Procedure for Processing Complaint

1. Post notice of policy (including prohibitions of harassment by ANY employees)
2. Complaint:
   a. made to proper department/party
   b. made to supervisory personnel and referred to proper department or party
   c. Re: advances/harassment by supervisors
   d. Re: advances/harassment by co-workers (based on racial-epithet cases)
3. Investigation
   a. Interview with complainant
   b. Interview with accused
   c. Check of personnel files
      i. Evidence of prior friction between parties
      ii. Previous complaints
      iii. Work records
   d. Interviews with witnesses/possible witnesses
4. Action to be taken
   a. No foundation other than complaint
      i. No record in accused's file; no dissemination of charge
      ii. Reiteration of policy against harassment; general announcement
   b. Some foundation
      i. Warning/notation in file
      ii. Warning/disciplinary slip
         • Warning coupled with automatic suspension upon second complaint
         • Reprimand coupled with automatic suspension upon second complaint
         • Reprimand/threat of suspension
   c. Solid foundation for charge
      i. Demotion
      ii. Suspension

iii. Dismissal

iv.   Restoration of work record of complaining employee

Remember: Fast corrective action will limit or eliminate your liability.

Drug Policy # 1

We are committed to helping all of our employees succeed in their new careers with (Employer) and strive to do everything possible to ensure the safety and well-being of our employees. In this connection and to avoid any possible problems in the future, I feel it is important to clearly communicate the attached policy regarding alcohol, drugs or controlled substances to all employees.

For the well-being of our employees we consider this to be a very serious matter and want you to understand that any violations of this policy may lead to immediate termination. Additionally, please keep in mind that federal and state laws may require the company to notify law enforcement agencies of certain violations.

Consistent with our desire to help every employee, we urge anyone who recognizes that they have a habit or problem which may be in violation of this policy to inform a member of management of their situation. In these cases we will work with the employee to encourage rehabilitation.

With the quality of the work force that we have at (Employer), we do not anticipate any problems; however, it is clearly to the benefit of everyone that there be no misunderstandings in such a crucial area. If you have any questions, please contact your supervisor.

Company President

Company Policy on Alcohol, Drugs and Controlled Substances #2

It is the company's policy to maintain a safe, productive working environment for everyone, and to safeguard company property. As part of this policy, the company prohibits the use, sale, transfer or possession of alcohol, drugs or controlled substances on any company premises or work sites. In addition, the company prohibits any employee from being at work under the influence of alcohol, drugs or controlled substances. The company also prohibits any visitor, contractor, or employee of any contractor from being on company premises or work sites while under the influence of alcohol, drugs or controlled substances. For purposes of this policy the following definitions are applicable:

Alcohol. Alcohol includes all intoxicating beverages that contain alcohol, including beer and wine.

Drugs and Controlled Substances. Drugs and controlled substances include all substances not prescribed by a licensed physician for use by the person possessing them. The company will determine at its sole discretion what is a drug or controlled substance. Any questions about whether or not a substance is a drug or controlled substance should be directed to your supervisor.

Anyone taking a drug or other medication, whether or not prescribed by the employee's physician for medical conditions, which is known or advertised as possibly affecting or impairing judgment, coordination, or other senses or which may adversely affect the ability to perform work in a safe and productive manner, must notify his or her supervisor or other management official prior to starting work in any of the company's facilities. The supervisor or management official will decide if the employee can remain at work on the company's premises or work site and what work restrictions, if any, are deemed necessary.

In order to ensure that each individual is provided a safe workplace, the company reserves the right to conduct searches or inspections of employees and their personal effects and vehicles located on the company's premises. These searches may be made without prior warning and may be conducted with the assistance of electronic devices, search dogs and representatives of law enforcement agencies. The company may require that an individual may at any time be required to give a urine or blood sample in order to determine compliance with this policy. A refusal to provide a sample means that there is a presumption of a violation of this policy. Any employee who violates or refuses to comply with this policy may be disciplined, including discharged.

Visitors or contractors who come onto the company premises are also subject to all provisions of this policy. We are committed to helping all of our employees succeed in their new careers with (employer) and strive to do everything possible to ensure the safety and well-being of our employees. In this connection, and to avoid any possible problems in the future, I feel it is important to clearly communicate the attached policy regarding alcohol, drugs or controlled substances to all employees.

For the well-being of our employees, we consider this to be a very serious matter and want you to understand that any violations of this policy may lead to immediate termination. Additionally, please keep in mind that federal and state laws may require the company to notify law enforcement agencies of certain violations.

Consistent with our desire to help every employee, we urge anyone who recognizes that they have a habit or problem which may be in violation of this policy to inform a member of management of their situation. In these cases we will work with the employee to encourage rehabilitation.

With the quality of the work force that we have at (employer), we do not anticipate any problems; however, it is clearly to the benefit of everyone that there be no misunderstandings in such a crucial area. If you have any questions, please contact your supervisor.

Company President

Employee Absenteeism Policy

You are expected to report for work on time on a regular basis. Unnecessary absenteeism and lateness is expensive, disruptive, and places an unfair burden on other employees and your supervisor.

Unsatisfactory attendance will also result in disciplinary action, including suspension and discharge. It will also have an adverse effect on any promotional considerations.

If you are going to be late or absent for any reason, telephone as far in advance of your starting time as possible. Explain why you are going to be absent and when you expect to return to work.

Note: It is your responsibility to ensure that proper notification is given. Asking another employee, friend, or relative to give this notification is not considered proper, except under emergency conditions.

Any employee who fails to give such notification will be charged with an unexcused absence. If an employee is absent for three (3) consecutive days without notifying the company, he or she is subject to discharge. If notice is given and the company does not think it justifies the absence, it will be considered unexcused. The following chart shows the discipline that will be administered for unexcused absences:

1st absence–Written Warning
2nd absence–Three-day Suspension
3rd absence–Ten-day Suspension
4th absence—Discharge

Three (3) consecutive unexcused absences—Discharge

Repeated lateness will also subject an employee to discipline including suspension and discharge.

Overtime: An employee may be excluded from overtime work during the week in which an unexcused absence occurs.

Suggested Procedure for Promotion and Transfer

1. Whenever possible, new and vacant positions will be filled from within the company by promoting qualified employees in conformity with the following:

   a. Employees of a department in which a vacancy occurs will be give priority over employees from another department for promotion to a position in that department.

   b. Promotions will be made on the basis of qualifications and merit as determined by a department head.

   c. Length of continuous service will be considered in promotions when it is the only significant difference among employees with equal or nearly equal qualifications.

2. If there are no employees within the company qualified to fill a vacancy, the best qualified applicant will be selected.

Promotion or Transfer – Interdepartmental

1. Employees in another department may be contacted regarding interdepartmental promotion or transfers only after permission is obtained from the employee's department head.

2. Employees promoted or transferred from one section or department to another section or department will not be considered as having broken their service in the computation of their length of employment for employee benefits.

3. Employees promoted or transferred from one section or department to another section or department will have their vacation allowance for the period concerned computed on the basis of the amount of vacation time earned in each position worked.

4. In cases in which a department would be seriously affected by the loss of employees who are to be promoted

or transferred, the department head may request a delay in the promotion or transfer providing the employees are so informed and the delay is not of such a duration as to cause them to lose their promotional or transfer opportunity. Delays will not generally exceed two weeks from the time the parties involved agree to the transfer, except upon agreement between the department heads concerned.

Transfer by Employee Request

1. An employee may request a transfer from an occupation or department to another occupation or department. Such a request need not be in the nature of a promotion. Requests for transfer must be made first to an employee's department head who will refer the employee to the Human Resources Department to determine his or her suitability for transfer.
2. An employee's request for transfer will be considered, except in unusual circumstances, only after he or she has been employed for at least six months in a position.
3. An employee's request for transfer will be considered on the basis of his or her qualifications for another position, his or her best interest, and those of the company.

Transfer for Company Convenience

1. Intra-departmental transfers of employees for a short duration for a company convenience may be at any time at the discretion of the department head providing the employee is informed of the need and expected duration of the transfer and it does not adversely affect the pay and benefits of the employee.
2. Interdepartmental transfers of employees for the company's convenience may be made by the department heads involved providing the employee is informed of the expected duration of the transfer and it does not adversely affect his or her pay and benefits.

Promotion from Within

1. As a matter of sound human resources practice, the following is established for filling higher level positions by promoting qualified employees. Eligible employees, as described in General Rules, paragraph "1" below, will be given the opportunity to apply for an open position in the following manner:

   a. All open positions that represent a promotion, as described in General Rules, under "A" will be posted on all department bulletin boards and distributed to department heads weekly.

   b. Preference for consideration for the listed positions will be given in the following order:

      i. Those employees within the work group where the opening exists.

      ii. Those employees within the department where the opening exists.

      iii. Those employees in related occupational groups outside the department where the opening exists and who would require minimal transitional training.

      iv. Those employees from any department in the company whose previous training, experience, education, attitude and seniority would seem to warrant whatever expenditure of training time and effort that may be required.

      v. In the event there are two or more employees whose qualifications are relatively equal, seniority will be a major consideration in the selection decision.

      vi. In the event there are no qualified applicants in the above categories, the Human Resources Department will recruit applicants from outside sources. To insure that company employees receive proper consideration for promotional opportunities, outside applicants for posted positions will not be considered until at least one week has elapsed from the time the Human Resources Department receives the requisition for a new employee.

General Rules for Promotion

To be considered for a promotion to a posted position (those that could not be filled through interdepartmental promotion), an employee must:

- apply for a posted position that represents a promotion of at least one classification; or, if the posted position does not represent an immediate promotion in classification, the position does offer the employee the opportunity to advance from one classification to another in a position hierarchy within a department through training and experience, e.g., from laborer to operator to lead person. Assuming that qualified candidates are available within the departments where such hierarchies exist, adherence to the "Promotion From Within Policy" will mean that the HR Department will receive requisitions for only the lower classifications;

- have completed _____ weeks of employment with the company;

- have been in their present position for at least six months;

- be carried on the rolls either as a permanent full-time employee or a permanent part-time employee who works 20 hours or more per week;

- have notified his present department head or supervisor of his intention to apply for a promotion and have filed the application for promotion form with the Employment Specialist in the HR Department.

Procedure

1. The Promotion From Within procedure will allow any employee the right to inquire, without prejudice, at the

Human Resources Department, about the requirements of the listed positions prior to notification of his present supervisor as specified in General Rules "A" and "(4)."

2. Before referring an employee to a department head for consideration for promotion, the Human Resources Department will interview the applicant to determine the motivation for, and the suitability of, the application; examine the applicant's background and work history; and elicit an opinion from the present supervisor as to work habits, attitude, etc.

3. The Human Resources Department will do everything necessary with both the applicant and department to assure an accurate presentation of the position requirements to the applicant and transmittal of applicant credentials to the department where the opening exists.

4. Department from which the successful applicant for promotion is chosen will arrange for the release of the employee to the new department within three weeks after being notified of the selection. This period may be extended by mutual agreement of the two department heads affected and the Director of Human Resources.

5. Promoted employees will have a one-month probationary period in the new job.

6. If at any time during the one-month probationary period the new department head decides that the employee is not suitable for the work he/she has been promoted to, the employee will be offered an available position in the company for which he/she is qualified and which carries the same grade that he/she held prior to transfer. The offered position will not necessarily be the same as the one held before promotion.

Abbreviations

WHT: White (not of Hispanic origin): ALL persons having origins in any of the original peoples of Europe, North Africa and the Middle East.

BLK: Black (not of Hispanic origin): ALL persons having origins in any of the Black racial groups.

HSP: Hispanic: ALL persons of Mexican, Puerto Rican, Cuban, Central or South American, or other Spanish culture or origin, regardless of race.

API: Asian or Pacific Islanders: ALL persons having origins in any of the original peoples of the Far East, Southeast Asia, or the Pacific Islands. This area includes, for example, China, Japan, Korea, the Philippine Islands, Samoa and the Indian subcontinent. [Areas comprising the Indian subcontinent include Bangladesh, Bhutan, India, Nepal, Pakistan, Sikkim, and Sri Lanka.]

NAT: American Indian or Alaskan Native: ALL persons having origins in any of the original peoples of North America.

EEO Classification Definitions

Officials and Managers–Occupations requiring administrative personnel who set broad policies, exercise overall responsibility for execution of these policies, and direct individual departments or special phases of a firm's operations.

Professional–Occupations requiring either college graduation or experience of such kind and amount as to provide a comparable background.

Technicians–Occupations requiring a combination of basic scientific knowledge and manual skill which can be obtained through about two years of post high school education, such as is offered in many technical institutes and junior colleges or through equivalent on the job training.

Office and Clerical–Includes all clerical-type work regardless of level of difficulty, where the activities are predominantly non-manual though some manual work not directly involved is included.

Operatives (semi-skilled)–Workers who operate machine or processing equipment or perform other factory-type duties of intermediate skill level which can be mastered in a few weeks and require only limited training.

Glossary of Terms

Affected Class: Members of a covered group who, because of past discrimination, continue, in the present, to suffer the effects of that discrimination.

Affirmative Action: The responsibility of an employer to take positive, concrete steps to expand employment opportunities for individuals in protected groups.

Affirmative Action Program: A detailed analysis of the employer's utilization of employees in protected categories and the company's goals and timetables to remedy any identified underutilization.

Applicant: An individual who can be identified by race and sex applying for a job for the first time during the affirmative action year.

Availability: Term applied in Affirmative Action Plans, to the incidence, in the labor market, or minorities and/or females with at least minimum qualifications (or qualifiability) for given jobs. Availability date is derived, for Affirmative Action Plans, from data contained in publications of the nearest State Employment Security Commission office.

BFOQ (Bona Fide Occupational Qualifications): Any authentic, substantive and job-related requirement used to determine a person's fitness for that job. Contractor identified, or claimed, BFOQ 's are subject to review by the U.S. Department of Labor, which takes a very narrow view of such claims.

Burden of Proof: The obligation on the party alleging discrimination to prove a preponderance of the evidence that discrimination took place.

Business Necessity: An employer's defense to a charge of disparate impact discrimination. To utilize this defense successfully, the employer must demonstrate a compelling business justification for perpetuating a practice that adversely impacts protected groups.

Charging Party: The individual filing a charge of discrimination with a state or federal discrimination agency.

Class Action: A lawsuit brought by an individual on behalf of himself and similarly situated individuals, *i.e.*, minority applicants not hired, not promoted.

Complainant: The individual filing a charge of discrimination with a state or federal discrimination agency (same as Charging Party).

Concentration: Term applied to a minority or female incumbency in a job that is disparate on the high side. Utilization at more than 120 percent availability is considered concentration.

Consent Decree: A court approved settlement agreement between the EEOC or an aggrieved party and the company. Such an agreement, because it is court approved, is like a judgment and is enforceable in the courts.

Constructive Discharge: The termination of an employee without express termination by making conditions so onerous that he/she quits.

Covered Group: Refers to minorities and/or females. They are the ones whom discriminatory actions have adversely affected. Order #4 "covers" them by making utilization in work force the prime topic of concern.

Deferral Agencies (706 Agencies): State, county and city discrimination agencies recognized by the Equal Employment Opportunity Commission as the agency with primary jurisdiction for discrimination cases in their locales.

Departmental (Organizational Unit) Analysis: Listing, by race and sex, of the jobs, rank ordered low to high (or in progression line order), including first line supervision, in each department (or similar organizational unit), such analysis to be inclusive of all person, jobs and departments (organizational units) in the facility or plant covered by an AAP.

Desk Audit: A government contractor's or subcontractor's response to the Office of Federal Contract Compliance request for a review of the company's progress in its affirmative action obligation.

Disparate Impact: Job qualifications or policies that appear to be neutral but that adversely impact on protected classifications e.g., Blacks, Hispanics.

Disparate Treatment: Treating or evaluating a protected employee in a manner different than a non-protected employee for the same type of conduct or job.

EEOC Guidelines: Interpretations by the Equal Employment Opportunity Commission of the discrimination laws which, although not in actuality statutory or case law, carries, in many instances, the weight of law.

EE0-1 Job Category: Name given to each of the nine work force subdivisions used in preparing Standard Form 100 (EE0-1) reports. The EE0-1 category names are Officials and Managers, Professionals, Technicians, Sales Workers, Office and Clerical, Craftspeople, Operatives, Laborers, and Service Workers.

Employment Offer: An expressed willingness to hire a specific person for a specific position at a specific rate of pay.

Equal Employment Opportunity Commission: A federal administrative agency created to police the Civil Rights Law of 1964 (Title VII).

Executive Orders: Presidential directives having the force and effect of law. These laws cover most government contractors and subcontractors.

Fact Finding Conference: A meeting conducted by an Equal Employment Opportunity Commission specialist, participated in by the charging party and the company. At these meetings each side is offered the opportunity to present its respective position. This conference is informal; statements are not made under oath and no official transcript is prepared.

Fair Employment Practice Laws: State laws pertaining to discrimination. Forty-eight states have such laws in either basic or comprehensive form.

Focus Job Titles: Name applied to a job having a concentration or underutilization. Name implies "problem" status requiring remedy.

Goals: Realistic, measurable, attainable objectives to be achieved through implementation and application of the Affirmative Action Plan. Generally, goals are:

1. Numerical Goals which represent those persons, minority and/or female, placement of whom is to be accomplished during an AAP year.

2. Annual Placement Rate Goals are expressed as percentages which, when applied to placement actions (hire, promotion, transfer), will produce achievement of ultimate goals.

3. Ultimate Goals are specific, measurable, attainable, results-oriented actions to eliminate problems impeding prompt and full utilizations of minorities and/or females at all levels and in all segments of a work force.

Good Faith Effort: Documentable action taken in pursuit of Affirmative Action Plan goals. Connotes practical, goal oriented, positive action, purposefully undertaken. Also used when assessing reasonable accommodation under the ADA.

Job Group: One of a group of jobs within an EE0-1 category, having similar (1) content (general type of duties), (2) wage rate, (3) opportunity (for training, mobility, potential for advancement, inherent in the job(s), not the person).

Job Relatedness: The connection between the requirements of the job and the factors relied on in selecting persons to fill the job.

Job Title, Job Classification: The name of a job; usually applied as the short identifier for a specific regimen of duties performed by employee for compensation.

National Labor Relations Board (NLRB): Federal Agency charged with administering the National Labor Relations Act (NLRA)

New Hire: The initial individual accession to the employer's rolls during an affirmative action year. Includes re-hires, and recalls if previously counted as terminations, but not reinstatements from leave absences.

Office of Federal Contract Compliance Programs (OFCCP): A department within the Department of Labor created to police all Executive Orders pertaining to employment and employment related policies of federal contractors and subcontractors.

On-Site Investigation: An investigator from the office of Federal Contract Compliance or other state or federal agency coming into the facility to inspect the records of a federal contractor or subcontractor; or a state fair employment agency representative coming into the facility with permission from the employer to investigate a charge of discrimination.

OPI: Opportunity Index: Simple numerical comparison which, when made, includes an arithmetic correlation that can be compared to an ideal of one, or parity. May be called adverse effect analysis.

Plan Year: The period of time, not to exceed 12 months, covered by an Affirmative Action Plan.

Prima Facie: The charging party's ability to set out the basic elements necessary to make out a claim of discrimination.

Promotion: The movement of an individual to another job classification of greater responsibility and/or greater pay. May or may not result in change of "category" placement on a subsequent EE0-1 Report. Promotions from one category to another should be recorded as occurring in the category from which the individual was promoted.

Promotion Offer: An expressed willingness to move a specific individual to another job title of greater responsibility and/or greater pay.

Protected Employees: Those employees who are covered under one or more discrimination laws. Employees in the following groups are protected: race, national origin, sex, age, handicapped, Vietnam-era veterans and disabled veterans.

Settlement Agreement: Agreement between the aggrieved party and company that is approved by state or federal discrimination agencies and resolves the charge of discrimination. This can also be a private agreement between the parties.

Sexual Harassment: A form of sex discrimination wherein sex or the request for sexual favors is made a condition of employment, *i.e.*, an offensive atmosphere is created.

Standard Metropolitan Statistical Area (SMSA): The population of a city and surrounding communities in which a plant is located for purposes of comparing racial make-up and sex of the normal recruiting area verses the racial and sexual make-up of the work force.

Systemic Action: An investigation into the entire organization (system) as a result of the belief by the Equal Employment Opportunity Commission that serious violations of the equal employment law exist throughout the organization.

Termination: The initial individual separation for any reasons from the employer's rolls. Includes layoffs, involuntary and voluntary separations, or death.

Timetable: The calendar-based schedule upon which AAP goal commitments are to be accomplished.

Title VII: Another name for the Civil Rights Act of 1964 and so named because it is the seventh article in 18 articles under the Civil Rights Act of 1964.

Trainee: Any employee enrolled in or who has completed (in the plan year) a formal, or informal, work related training course, of any length, on or off the employer's premises. Such training is that, generally, which qualifies an employee for employment above the entry level.

Training Offer: An expressed willingness to enroll a specific employee in a specific work related training course, formal or informal, of any length, on or off the employer's premises.

Transfer: A personnel action which does not immediately increase wages, but provides the opportunity for greater advancement in a different career area.

Underutilization: A smaller percentage of minorities or females in the work force in relation to the availability of same in the recruiting area.

Utilization Analysis: A comparison of the racial/sexual make-up of the city and surrounding communities versus the employer's work force.

Validation: Proving through statistical analysis that a job test accurately measures the ability to perform the job for which a test was given.

ABOUT THE AUTHOR

Thom K. Cope graduated with honors from Syracuse University in 1969 with a B.A. and received his Juris Doctor in 1972 from the University of Nebraska College of Law. For over 40 years, he has practiced law in the area of employment discrimination, management relations, and was the Vice President of Human Resources for a large company in Tucson, Arizona. His practice emphasizes employment relations law in all phases from administrative matters, National Labor Relation Board matters to federal and state trials. As an experienced mediator, Mr. Cope mediates all types of employment disputes.

Mr. Cope is admitted to practice in Arizona, Nebraska, California, the U.S. Supreme Court, and various Circuit Courts of Appeals. He has practiced in San Francisco, New York City, Lincoln, Nebraska and Tucson, Arizona. Cope is listed in *Who's Who in American Law, Who's Who in the East, The Best Lawyers in America, Southern Arizona Super Lawyers* and *Arizona's Finest Lawyers*.

He was appointed a Judge of the Commission of Industrial Relations in 1985 and served for six years. He is a Fellow of the College of Labor and Employment Law. Mr. Cope was a member of the Nebraska Supreme Court Gender Fairness Task Force. He has lectured extensively to managers and supervisors throughout the United States in the area of equal employment law and management practices. *The Executive Guide to Employment Practices,* 1st edition, was a featured selection in Macmillan's Executive Book of the Month Club.

He has also been a visiting professor at Nebraska Wesleyan University, an adjunct Labor Law professor at Pima Community College and an instructor in business law, management, and the U.S. Constitution at the University of Phoenix in Tucson, Arizona. Mr. Cope authored the The Age Discrimination and Employment Act section of *The Arizona Employment Law Handbook,* 2013 Supplement.

Mr. Cope obtained national certification as a Senior Professional in Human Resources (SPHR) for six years.

He is currently a partner at the Mesch, Clark & Rothschild law firm in Tucson, Arizona.

Mr. Cope can be reached at tcope@mcrazlaw.com.